TOM GLOVER

'No shortcuts to spiritual maturity'

Biblical BOOKS

A Life Worth Living
© Copyright February 2011 Tom Glover
Email: thomashglover@btinternet.com

ISBN 978-1-905989-43-0

Except where stated, Scripture quotations are from The Holy Bible:
New International Version, © International Bible Society, 1973, 1978, 1984.

Biblical
BOOKS

JC Print Ltd, Belfast
Telephone: 0786020533
Fax: 028 9079 0420
Email: info@jcprint.net

Dedication

With lots of love to our grandsons
Matthew and Reuben
and granddaughter Charlie.

A word of appreciation ...

I am indebted to the following people for their
contribution towards the writing of this book:

My wife, Dorothy, and my family for their
continual support and encouragement.

Dr William Thomson who oversaw this book
and Margaret Maxwell for her assistance in proof reading.
Both have also been a great source of encouragement.

Foreword

This book is for all who want to deepen their Christian faith and who want to enter into the fulness of what it means to know and walk with Christ. The Apostle Paul urged all believers in Christ: *Let your roots grow down into him and draw nourishment from him, so that you will grow in faith, strong and vigorous in the truth* (Colossians 2:7 NLT).

This book will help the modern-day disciple of Christ fulfil their desire to grow in love and knowledge of Christ. It is not a heavy or difficult book, intended for people with degrees in divinity; it is readable and practical, yet not lightweight. It is a challenging, plain speaking call to wholehearted commitment to Christ.

It is often said that the best and quickest way to learn is from one who has both knowledge and experience. This is true whether we are at the elbow of a craftsman or in the lecture room of an experienced scholar. Tom Glover has lived out the Christian life in all kinds of circumstances for many years. I have watched him grow in his knowledge of and love for Christ; I have seen him mature as a servant of Christ ... first, as a mature student at Bible College, then as an evangelist and, finally, as a pastor of three churches in Scotland.

This journey was undertaken against a background of illness in the family. As a longstanding friend and confidante, I have witnessed the inside story and I have seen a sincere and genuine faith lived out, tried and tested. Tom has applied the truths in this book to his own life and I am so glad that he is passing them on to a new generation. Echoing the words of 1 Peter 1:7, Tom's faith has proved genuine and it reflects honour and glory to the Christ whom he serves.

I believe that Tom Glover is well placed to write such a helpful and accessible book on discipleship – how to grow as a Christian. Knowledge will be increased, faith deepened and love for Christ strengthened if this book is read and applied to life. It is a joy and a privilege to commend this useful tool for developing Christian maturity.

Rev Stuart Wadsworth

A word from the author ...

In his book, *The Normal Christian Life*, Watchman Nee (1903-1972), a well-known Chinese evangelist and author who suffered much for his faith, writes: 'What is the normal Christian life? It is something very different from the life of the average Christian.' His observations during the period in which he lived and ministered are much in evidence today. Most Christians, I suggest, but not judgmentally, are living below par. The supreme goal of all who seek to follow Christ must be to live 'a normal Christian life'. But what is meant by 'normal'?

The privilege of knowing God through his Son, Jesus, is immense and unparalleled. To experience the purpose of God, understand his will and live for his glory, is what mankind was created for. The late David Watson once said: 'The world around us is sick of words and starved of reality.' God's purpose for the Christian is to show this needy world that there is a life worth living.

The normal Christian life is making Christ visible in thought, word and deed. How far short many of us fall! This is a hard and narrow way, one of self-denial and commitment. The temptation to try and find an easy or quick route on this journey only leads to a lack of spiritual growth and frustration. Spiritual maturity can no more be produced overnight than apples growing on a tree. The Bible says nothing about shortcuts to spiritual maturity.

This book will help the believer understand what the Bible has to say about living a life for the glory of God – to walk and live in the Spirit, to know and experience the power and grace of God, even in the darkest days. God does not leave his children in ignorance, but through his Word and by his Spirit, he enables us to know the joy of complete commitment to Christ.

CONTENTS

PART 1   OBEDIENCE TO THE CALL OF JESUS

1. From the lips of Jesus – the challenge of self-denial
2. A change of allegiance
3. Your first love
4. Confessing your Saviour

PART 2   ENCOUNTERING THE HOLY SPIRIT

5. The Holy Spirit is God
6. Life begins with birth
7. Filled with the Spirit
8. Walking in the Spirit
9. Empowered by the Spirit
10. Transformed by the Spirit

PART 3   GOD'S PURPOSE FOR YOU

11. Worship
12. The power of humility
13. Continuing steadfastly
14. Discovering God's will
15. Pathway to holiness

1

From the lips of Jesus – the challenge of self-denial

As Jesus travelled through the Galilean countryside with his disciples, he captured the attention of vast crowds who followed him. They had never heard anyone speak like him or seen anyone do the miraculous things he did, even raising the dead ... *Nothing like this has ever been seen in Israel* (Matthew 9:33). His heart went out to them! *When he saw the crowds he had compassion on them, because they were harassed and helpless, like sheep without a shepherd* (Matthew 9:36). Jesus, however, was in no doubt at all that amidst this vast number there would have been the inquisitive, the critics, the troubled, and those who were sincerely seeking.

How did Jesus respond to them? What words were suitable for such a large mixed gathering? What did they need to hear more than anything else? Knowing that the way ahead for those who would become his followers would not be easy, Jesus, with the authority he possessed as the Son of God, laid down the radical challenge of discipleship. Following Jesus was not for the fainthearted or those merely emotionally stirred. It called for serious consideration.

And so, Jesus said to them: *If anyone would come after me ...* (Mark 8:34-35). His challenge was conditional and without prejudice, it was to all present. The words *come after* mean to 'attach oneself'. The inference, at that time, meant more than just accepting Jesus' teaching, but to literally follow him wherever he went. The word *if* indicates the need for careful thought, avoiding impulsive decisions. This point is made clear from Matthew 8:18-22 where a couple of would-be disciples show their eagerness without first having counted the cost. Jesus laid down two requirements for those who wanted to become his disciples.

Firstly, *he must deny himself.* C E B Cranfield writes: 'To deny oneself is to disown, not just one's sins, but one's self, to turn away from the idolatry of self-centredness.' So it is something much more radical than any mere ascetic or trivial self-denials. It is essentially saying 'No' to self, our ego and pride, our wants and wishes, our self-glorifying dreams and ambitions. Self-denial calls for the complete surrender of every thought, word and deed. This is not easy; it is outright warfare between the flesh and the Spirit, for the pull of our sinful nature is powerful and not compatible with the purpose of God (cf. Romans 8:5-8).

Counting the cost can also mean saying 'No' to much in life that is not necessarily sinful, but which may be a hindrance or disadvantage in the pursuit of true discipleship. In Hebrews 12:1-2 the author affirms this point when he writes: *Let us throw off everything that hinders and the sin that so easily entangles, and let us run with perseverance the race marked out for us.* Garibaldi, the great Italian patriot, appealed for recruits with these words: 'I offer no pay, nor quarters, nor provisions; I offer hunger, thirst, forced marches, battles and death. Let him who loves his country in his heart, and not with lips only, follow me.' Demanding, this challenge may be; however, the joy of obeying the call of God and seeking to live daily for the glory of God is more than reward enough.

The second requirement was to *take up his cross and follow me*. In this narrative there are two crosses, one that belonged to Jesus and the other which belonged to those who would follow him. What did this mean? At that period in history, many criminals were punished for their crimes by crucifixion, and had to carry their own cross to the place of execution. It was a one way journey. There was no way back. Self no longer mattered, future plans became obsolete – the cross meant the end for self.

Unlike the person being crucified and carrying his cross under duress, the follower of Jesus would carry his cross because he wants to, not because he must. It is an act of willing surrender and love for Jesus. It involves a life of trust (John 14:1), walking in Jesus' footsteps (1 Peter 2:21), obeying Jesus' commands (John 15:14), and continuing (Philippians 2:12).

After introducing his readers to some wonderful doctrinal truths in his letter to the Christians at Rome, the Apostle Paul challenged them to make their response in light of all that Christ had done for them. He writes: *Therefore, I urge you, brothers, in view of God's mercy, to offer your bodies as living sacrifices, holy and pleasing to God ...* (Romans 12:1). In other words, since Christ has shown you mercy by the complete giving of himself on the cross, the very least you can do in response is to offer back to him all that you are and have in an act of complete surrender! In the Old Testament, when animals were sacrificed as an offering for sin they were completely slain, rendered lifeless! The challenge to those who follow Christ must be equally as complete, but with one main difference, they must be *living* – a living sacrifice!

Following the denial of self and the taking up of our cross, there must be the continual self-giving of every fibre of our being. This should not be seen as a one-off wonder, rather, it's a lifetime of commitment borne out of a deep sense of love and gratitude. In Galatians 2:20 Paul tells us how he felt: *I have been crucified with Christ and I no longer live, but Christ lives in me. The life I live in the body, I live by faith in the Son of God, who loved me and gave himself for me.*

In John 15:18, Jesus taught his disciples that just as the world hated him so, likewise, those who followed him could expect nothing less. Those who would follow Jesus should not expect an easy journey through life because they followed in the footsteps of the Master. In Mark 8:35, we have a great paradox: *For whoever wants to save his life will lose it, but whoever loses his life for me and for the gospel will save it.*

The challenge of discipleship now takes on board the concept of investment. Saving one's life in this context refers to living according to one's own passion, desire and will; in other words, living a life independent of the purpose of God. When a person invests in such a way, it is viewed, according to Jesus, as a life that is lost and wasted, for its value is limited to their earthly life. On the other hand, the life surrendered to Jesus and his gospel is a life invested in the eternal kingdom of God. Such an investment involves sacrifice and commitment, yet it's one of fulfilment and eternal reward.

In John 12:24, Jesus said: *I tell you the truth, unless a grain of wheat falls into the ground and dies, it remains only a single seed. But if it dies, it produces many seeds.* The picture is clear! The seed that is planted in the earth dies but, as a result, it produces many seeds. It has been a great investment! Paradoxically, the death of the old self-life is more the beginning than the end. The ultimate and highest example is surely that of Jesus' own death on the cross. As a result of his death, countless men and women would come to faith.

From Isaiah 53:10b, the result of Christ's death is recorded prophetically: *The plan was that he give himself as an offering for sin so that he would see life come from it – life, life, and more life. And God's plan will deeply prosper through him* (The Message, Eugene H Peterson). The true value of discipleship is further stressed by Jesus in Mark 8:36-37 where he made it clear that even if a person possessed all this world's treasures he would still be in spiritual poverty if that is all he has, because he has forfeited or neglected the priority of his soul.

The pathway to a life worth living which will glorify God and bring total fulfilment and soul satisfaction must begin with our complete surrender to Jesus Christ as our Lord and Saviour. Wanting only what he wants, and by finding great pleasure through pleasing him. Only then can we fulfil the purpose for which God created us. The Apostle Paul writes in 2 Corinthians 5:9 that *we make it our goal to please him.* If our aim is for self-exaltation, public prominence or recognition and if our desire is to make our mark before others, we have missed the mark! Surely, John the Baptist got it right when he said: *[Jesus Christ] must become greater; I must become less* (John 3:30).

The beginning for all those who would become true disciples and followers of Jesus is to respond to his call with active obedience. This is only the start of a journey which requires continual trust and commitment ... for there is no easy way, no shortcuts to spiritual maturity.

2
A change of allegiance

So long as we live on this earth we shall never be completely free from the tyranny of self. The inward struggle between the old and the new life will always be in competition, vying for first place. This is to be expected and is not a problem in itself. The difficulty arises when we allow our loyalties to remain with the old nature, that is, doing what we want, thinking what we like, and obeying our own natural sinful instincts.

Many Christians never grow into spiritual maturity because they have not moved on from their initial belief ... consequently, they remain spiritual babies. Yes, they are saved, having repented, sought forgiveness and received Christ into their lives through faith, but their allegiance remains towards self. They want to manage their own lives. Settling for just being saved without growing in Christ was never God's purpose. Some Christians at Corinth had not grown up – they knew Christ but had never progressed – they were worldly, so Paul had to write: *Brothers, I could not address you as spiritual but worldly – mere infants in Christ. I gave you milk, not solid food, for you were not yet ready for it* (1 Corinthians 3:1-2). The Apostle Peter writes: *But grow in the grace and knowledge of our Lord Jesus Christ* (2 Peter 3:18).

Battles must be fought and victories won if spiritual growth is to take place, but this requires our allegiance to Christ not just as Saviour, but also as Lord. There are so many areas in life that call for Christ to be Lord ... work, family, leisure, relationships, finance, church life and worship are but a few. He must have our total allegiance. We must decide who has first place in our hearts.

Christ must reign supreme, not alongside anyone or anything else. He is to have no equal! He alone must be seated on the throne of the believer's heart ... *In your hearts set apart Christ as Lord* (1 Peter 3:15). Compromise and middle ground is not an option. The one who freely gave himself up for us deserves all that we are and have. To the Colossian Christians, Paul wrote: *so that in everything, he might have the supremacy* (1:18).

The challenge of allegiance is to be found throughout God's Word. This is strikingly true of the Apostle Paul in Romans 7:7-25. In this section, Paul is honest with himself and his readers. He knew what was right to do, but found it difficult. As a result, he often failed: *For I have the desire to do what is good, but I cannot carry it out* (verse 18). He continually battled and struggled as the old and new natures clashed with each other.

Although he was honest about the warfare that raged within him, and not always able to bring his thoughts and deeds under control, he did not let failure have the final say. Later in this same letter (8:37), addressing the same Christians, he wrote: *No, in all these things we are more than conquerors through him who loved us.* Similarly, in Philippians, *I can do everything through him who gives me strength* (4:13).

The ongoing fight against our sinful nature is certain, but equally so is the victory for all God's children who turn to Christ for strength. There is wisdom in recognising our own weakness and inability for, in so doing, we can turn to Christ and his mighty power, hence Paul's insightful comment: *for my power is made perfect in weakness ... for when I am weak, then I am strong* (2 Corinthians 12:9-10).

Paul's experience is replicated in some measure in our own lives. We can all see something of ourselves in Paul's struggle against the sinful nature. How often, even when we have known what is right to say, think or do, have we failed, only to sense our disappointment or even disgust; sometimes left wallowing in our own misery and hearing those familiar words, 'Lord, not again!' The challenge of allegiance will never go away, but how reassuring it is to know that because of Christ's victory on the cross, we too can share in this victory as we take up our cross daily and follow him.

The parable of the lost son in Luke 15 is essentially about allegiance. The younger of two sons went to his father and asked for the portion of his father's inheritance that was due to him. His intention was to move away to another country, far from home, and do his own thing. He wanted to manage his own life and have the liberty and freedom to call the shots – he would do whatever he chose. This story is well documented.

The outcome of his strong self-will is summed up in verse 13 where we read that he *squandered all his wealth in wild living*. His whole life turned around, but not in the way he expected. From the security and abundance of life working with his father to a position of destitution and isolation; no friends, no food ... nothing! Perhaps the most telling words in this story are found in verse 17: *When he came to his senses.* He realised that he had messed things up and that doing his own thing wasn't such a good idea.

There are times when we can be rather headstrong, thinking we know better, and allow the pull of the old nature to lead us in wrong directions. Usually we haven't travelled too far when we recognise the error of our ways, just like the younger son. However, he decided to exercise humility and return to his father. Without stretching truths contained in this parable, learning to stay close to our heavenly Father and keeping focused on his purpose must be our singular goal.

In practical terms, this means daily surrendering to his will, allowing him to manage and direct our lives. His will in preference to ours! It's a question of trust! Just like the father in this parable, we too have a Father in heaven who never stops loving or caring and one who welcomes his wayward children with a forgiving embrace.

Sometimes we may try to justify our behaviour by saying, 'That's just the way I am' as though that makes it all right. The point is, however, it may not be the way God wants us to be. Resistance to change is an ever-present reality; the crucifying of the old life is painful, but profitable! In Paul's exhortation to the Christians at Colosse, he invited them to set their hearts on things above (3:1), then he provided practical instructions on how to deal with sin: *Put to death, therefore, what belongs to your earthly nature ...* (3:5). No compromise or half measures, but death to all that is sinful was Paul's advice.

Jonathan Edwards (1703-1758), the great philosopher/theologian said: 'I have this day been before God and have given myself – all that I have and am – to God; so that I am in no respect my own. I have given myself clean away.' That great man of faith, George Muller (1805-1898), when asked, 'What is the secret of your service for God' answered: 'There was a day when I died – died to George Muller, his opinions, preferences, tastes and will – died to the world, its approval or censure – died to the approval or blame of even my brethren or friends – since then I have studied to show myself approved only to God.'

Moment by moment, hour by hour, day by day, our allegiance to Christ will be tested. When temptation affords itself to us we must flee from it, neither dwelling nor pondering for a second, but heeding the words of James: *Submit yourselves, then, to God. Resist the devil, and he will flee from you. Come near to God and he will come near to you* (4:7-8). When tempted, even in the smallest thing, we must surrender ourselves afresh to God. It is not always a question of whether something is wrong or not, the question is: is it a help or hindrance in the kingdom of God? Will Christ be exalted? Will our thoughts and deeds bring glory to our Lord? Paul's charge to Timothy reads: *But you, man of God, flee from all this, and pursue righteousness, godliness, faith, love, endurance and gentleness* (1 Timothy 6:11).

The privilege of knowing God is immense, quite beyond human discernment! That God should express any interest in humankind is the measure of his grace and not our worth. Why did God breathe the breath of life into us? Why should he bother about us at all? The fact is, he loves us beyond measure and has privileged us by wanting his purpose to be worked out through us, mere sinners saved by grace! Believe it or not, God's redemptive glory actually becomes visible in his children when they take up their cross, and with his strength, seek to live the crucified life – thereby exalting the Lord Jesus – even becoming like him. *But thanks be to God, who always leads us in triumphal procession in Christ and through us spreads the fragrance of the knowledge of him. For we are the aroma of Christ ...* (2 Corinthians 2:14-15).

The challenge of allegiance is not restricted to the New Testament alone. In the Old Testament we find many of God's servants were similarly challenged. David and Daniel, prophets and priests, together with many others, leave us with lessons to learn as they at times struggled to give God his rightful place.

God's servant Joshua presented the Israelites with an ultimatum. Having had a history of success and failure, obedience and disobedience, Joshua laid down the gauntlet of allegiance when he said: *Now fear the Lord and serve him with all faithfulness ... choose for yourselves this day whom you will serve ... as for me and my household, we will serve the Lord* (Joshua 24:14-15). The people responded by saying for the second time: *We will serve the Lord* (verse 21).

God is looking for men and women today who will nail their colours to the mast and declare unequivocally in all things that Jesus Christ is Lord of their lives. C H Spurgeon (1834-1892) said: 'If the service of God is worth anything, it is worth everything.'

3

Your first love

Many years ago a young and promising artist decided to paint a portrait of Jesus. He took his time and put much thought and effort into it, applying all the principles and techniques he had been taught and had learned through his (limited) experience. Eventually, when his work was finished, he took it to a famous artist, a man of great repute, for his opinion. Without haste or hurry, he examined the portrait with the eye of a master, and then said to the young man: 'You do not love him, or you would have painted him better.' How telling! This begs the question for all who follow Jesus: to what extent is our love for him visible? What picture does our life paint of Christ?

Love is a well used word in our vocabulary. We use it in a great variety of ways – sometimes referring to people, things, events, or whatever, the list is endless. That God loves us is well documented throughout his Word. It is evident in the Old Testament in relation to his covenant people, Israel, who, in spite of their cyclic disobedience and waywardness, God kept loving. His love found expression through his patience towards them.

The cross, however, must remain the supreme expression of God's love for a lost world. The Apostle John writes: *This is how we know what love is: Jesus Christ laid down his life for us* (1 John 3:16). God's love for the world became visible through the gift of his Son on the cross. His love for us was sacrificial, complete and without measure – no gift could have been greater and no love could be deeper. The point is: the love of God was seen in action, it moved beyond words.

Likewise, evidence that we love God must be seen. Words can be cheap, they often come easy. To say that we love our Lord is mere hypocrisy unless our love for him is clear for all to see. This was the problem with the church at Ephesus. In Revelation 2:1-6, we have the words of Jesus himself addressed to this congregation. He wrote to them because they had lost their first love for him.

In his exhortation he paid them several fine compliments, indeed, there were seven – all recognising their hard work, their patient endurance, and their stand for the truth. Although this church was worthy of praise and commendation, like many churches today, there was one major deficiency ... they had lost their first love! They were no longer in love with the Lord Jesus the way they used to be.

They were busy and industrious, doing all the right things. There was no lack of prayer, giving, or serving. They were busy, but loveless! Jesus said: *Yet I hold this against you; you have forsaken your first love. Remember the height from which you have fallen!* (2:4-5). Their loveless state was so bad that Jesus presented them with only one course of action, when he said: *Repent and do the things you did at first* (verse 5). Jesus was saying: 'Fall in love with me again, just like you once did.' What a challenge!

Surely this is a timely word for God's people today! A church may be well established, prosperous and extremely busy, the notice board may be packed with activities, it may also have a great reputation before men, and even jealously admired by other churches. However, all this is meaningless if love for the Lord Jesus is absent.

According to 1 Corinthians 13:3, no matter how gifted or great in faith we are, even if we give ourselves up in martyrdom, but have not love – we are nothing. In Revelation 2:5, the importance of love is strengthened by the ultimatum given by Jesus: *If you do not repent, I will remove your lampstand from its place.* In other words, 'I will remove my presence from you.' It is clear throughout the New Testament that this was a problem for most churches, the following examples make this point:

- *This is my prayer that your love may abound more and more* (Philippians 1:9)
- *Follow the way of love* (1 Corinthians 14:1)
- *I urge you to reaffirm your love* (2 Corinthians 2:8)
- *Let us not love with words or tongue but with actions and truth* (1 John 3:18)
- *Live a life of love, just as Christ loved you* (Ephesians 5:2)

Why should this love be so crucial? Because *love never fails* (1 Corinthians 13:8). Somehow or other, in spite of all our weaknesses and failures, our smallness and seeming insignificance, where there is genuine love for the Lord Jesus, the presence and purpose of God becomes a living reality. We cannot manufacture it, we cannot work it up; if it's there we know it, but equally so, the absence of love cannot be hid, and we know it! In Romans 8:28, Paul brings the purpose of God and the believer's love for him together, when he writes: *And we know that in all things God works for the good of those who love him.*

Paul introduces 1 Corinthians 13 with these words: *And now I show you the most excellent way*, and begins the following chapter with *follow the way of love*. Love is, undoubtedly, the way of excellence. In this chapter, Paul defines love in the most comprehensive way; he does so by contrasting the gifts of the Spirit, wisdom, faith and prophecy, and also by accentuating the negative – what love is not (verses 4-7). Three words sum up the power and purpose of love in this passage, *love never fails* (verse 8).

In our relationships with both Christian and non-Christian people, love is the key. There is something about love which silences debate, discussion, and even rationality at times. In his short letter to Philemon, Paul wrote to encourage the believers to receive a slave called Onesimus (who had run away) into fellowship. During his time away he had been converted, and so Paul appeals to these believers to receive him back, not as a slave, but as a dear brother. And so, rather than attempt to prove the rights and wrongs of this situation, Paul simply says: *I appeal to you on the basis of love* (verse 9). Love is always a winner!

It is, however, important to understand that love must, firstly, be personal. True love for others will only be possible when we are personally in love with the Lord Jesus. One will flow from the other. This was the challenge the Apostle Peter faced. A great and mighty ministry lay ahead of him that would call for the complete surrender of his life. Peter was loud, daring, impulsive, and quick with words. He attempted things that his disciple companions would not. At times he failed only because he took risks.

Peter is remembered and often criticised unduly because he denied his Lord three times after pledging his allegiance for Jesus, even to the point of death. In Matthew 26:35, Peter said: *Even if I have to die with you, I will never disown you.* The part that is often forgotten is this: *And all the other disciples said the same.* Let us be careful not to judge!

Having denied his Lord three times, it is understandable that in John 21:15-19 Jesus presented Peter with a threefold challenge in relation to his love for him. Responding to the first two challenges, Peter said: *Yes, Lord, you know that I love you.* But for the third time, and almost with a sense of exasperation, he said: *Lord, you know all things; you know that I love you.* Now Peter was truly ready to be an apostle of Jesus Christ. Jesus simply said to him: *Follow me* (verse 19). Peter would live up to his words, eventually dying for his Lord; he really did love Jesus more than anything or anyone else. Are we able to say with Peter, *'Lord, you know all things; you know that I love you'*? How do we measure up to the command of our Saviour ... *Love the Lord your God with all your heart and with all your soul and with all your mind and with all your strength* (Mark 12:30).

The normal Christian life demands that we love Jesus more than anything else in life. This means that every day will be a day of communion with our Lord, no matter our activities, whatever our plans and usage of time. Whatever our hands find to do, whatever our thoughts and deeds, even how we spend our money, all must be done as an expression of our love for Jesus, and for the sake of his glory.

May God help us by his Spirit to sift us as wheat, revealing to us where our love is lacking and giving us grace, and showing us as never before the full expression of our Saviour's love for us so that in response, we too, will live the crucified life as an expression of our love for him.

4

Confessing your Saviour

CH Spurgeon (1834-1892), one of the greatest pastors and preachers of all time, who sought to share Christ and exalt his name with all of his being, wrote: 'As long as there is breath in our bodies, let us serve Christ; as long as we can think, as long as we can speak, as long as we can work, let us serve him, let us even serve him with our last gasp; and, if it be possible, let us try to set some work going that will glorify him when we are dead and gone. Let us scatter some seed that may spring up when we are sleeping beneath the hillock in the cemetery.'

Jesus called his disciples to follow him and share with him in his ministry of proclaiming the good news about himself. They had listened to him and looked on all that he did; they travelled together, ate and prayed together. Three years spent in Jesus' company was their learning and growing time before they themselves were commissioned by him, as apostles, to go into the world and preach the gospel ... *Therefore go and make disciples of all nations, baptising them in the name of the Father and of the Son and of the Holy Spirit, and teaching them to obey everything I have commanded you* (Matthew 28:19).

Just before Jesus' ascension into heaven, he said to them: *You will receive power when the Holy Spirit comes on you, and you will be my witnesses in Jerusalem, and in all Judea and Samaria, and to the ends of the earth* (Acts 1:8). From that moment on, men and women would come to faith in Christ, becoming the firstfruits of the New Testament church which began with the confession of Christ, and has continued to grow globally ever since.

The apostles were specially chosen men and their ministry was unique. Their apostleship died with them when they had fulfilled the purpose for which Christ chose them. However, the responsibility to preach the gospel and share the good news of Jesus Christ was passed on to the church, of which all believers are part. Although the public preaching of the Word is the primary means of proclaiming the truth of the gospel, every member of the church, which is the body of Christ, has the responsibility to confess Christ as their Saviour and Lord.

The significance of every believer individually confessing Christ or witnessing to his saving and keeping power must not be underestimated. Some time ago I conducted a survey among mature Christians with regard to the circumstances in which they came to know Christ. The results were both telling and encouraging. Six categories were used as a general guide:

- Church service   15%
- Evangelistic rally   17%
- Reading Bible or book   8%
- House Party or camp   18%
- On your own   10%
- Personal witness   32%

It has to be noted that the means whereby a person was influenced before ultimately making a commitment to Christ may not simply have been one directional; several of the above categories may have come into play. The point is, however, confessing Christ is both the Christian's responsibility and privilege. These statistics show us the value of the personal sharing of our faith.

Perhaps we should ask the question, 'What reasons do we have for confessing Christ?' It would be easy to say that we are commanded to confess Christ, and that our reason for so doing is one of obedience. Although this is commendable and true, it could come across as rather legalistic. So what other reasons could we have? How about gratitude! Paul writes: *For Christ's love compels us* (2 Corinthians 5:14). Unless we are deeply grateful for all that Christ has done for us, and been touched by his grace, forgiveness and love, we are unlikely to be motivated to share our experience of him with others.

However, in all our endeavours to confess Christ, we must always remember that the work of salvation belongs to God, we are merely the instruments. *What, after all, is Apollos? And what is Paul? Only servants, through whom you came to believe – as the Lord has assigned to each his task. I planted the seed, Apollos watered it, but God made it grow* (1 Corinthians 3:5-6).

There are those who have been given the gift of evangelism – it might be in public ministry, or on a one-to-one basis, or in some other specialised area. But this is not, however, our chief consideration. According to the New Testament, confessing our Saviour is the responsibility of all Christians. How are we to do this?

Like Moses, we may not feel eloquent (cf. Exodus 4:10), or it might be that we consider ourselves to be lacking in knowledge. Whatever our inadequacies (in our own eyes) may be, God delights to use us in our smallness and weakness so that the reality of Christ may shine through us. We don't have to preach sermons, wax eloquent or be an authority on evangelism and personal witness.

When the blind man who was healed in John 9 was quizzed by the religious authorities as to how and when he received his sight, he simply said: *One thing I do know. I was blind but now I see* (verse 9). He couldn't answer all the smart questions, but he was sure of one thing – he once was blind, and now he could see. His life had changed. Just a few words, but very powerful!

People may dispute our beliefs and theology, they may disagree with the Bible or even deny the existence of God, but they cannot deny the reality of a changed life! How are we to confess our Saviour? Jesus said: *You are the light of the world. A city on a hill cannot be hidden. Neither do people light a lamp and put it under a bowl. Instead they put it on its stand, and it gives light to everyone in the house. In the same way, let your light shine before men, that they may see your good deeds and praise your Father in heaven* (Matthew 5:14-16).

The power of a transformed life is telling! It gives off light and life, it shows purpose and direction. The life of Jesus, his character and nature, become a voice that cannot be denied – it is there for all to see. Normal Christian living takes place when through the transforming work of the Holy Spirit, Christ becomes visible, not just through our words, but also our life and lifestyle.

One of the greatest compliments ever paid to believers is found in 2 Corinthians 2:14-15 where believers are described as the aroma of Christ: *But thanks be to God, who ... through us spreads everywhere the fragrance of the knowledge of him. For we are to God the aroma of Christ among those who are being saved and those who are perishing.*

Confessing our Saviour begins with the evidence of a transformed life! Words without a changed life is hypocrisy! The story is told of a missionary who had been working in India for many years. During those years the local people had listened to his message and looked at his life, then one man was heard to say: 'If I am to believe in his Saviour, then he has to look more saved.'

Many wonderful lessons have been drawn from the fourth chapter of the Gospel of John. However, in keeping with our purpose and theme, there is something to learn from the Samaritan woman, following her conversation with Jesus. From a position of seeming ignorance regarding salvation, (which comes through faith in Jesus Christ) this woman (humanly speaking) made an incredible impact on many of the Samarians who lived in the town where she lived. We are informed in verse 39 that she gave her testimony. But what was her testimony? *He told me everything I ever did.*

The knowledge of her past and present life, as revealed by Jesus, together with the truth about salvation, had convinced her of her own need and who Jesus was. Some of the Samaritans who heard this woman confess Christ had become believers, others decided to seek out Jesus for themselves and invited him to stay with them, for we read that *they urged him to stay with them* (verse 40). As a result of this, we read: *And because of his words many more became believers* (verse 41).

We shall never know the full extent of this woman's simple testimony. She was not skilled, trained or theologically educated – she simply told her story! Those who listened to her were certainly convinced of the reality of her experience. They could not deny the change in her life!

In Mark 8:37-38 Jesus referred to a future occasion when he would personally return to earth with his holy angels. Having challenged the crowd around him regarding the commitment involved in following him, he said: *If anyone would come after me, he must deny himself and take up his cross and follow me ... then ... If anyone is ashamed of me and my words ... the Son of Man will be ashamed of him when he comes.* Jesus was saying that if anyone was too proud or fearful to confess him openly in this life, then he too will be ashamed of them when he returns; he will not confess them before his Father in heaven. In 2 Timothy 1:8, we read: *So do not be ashamed to testify about our Lord.*

The challenge brought before them was that of taking their stand for Jesus Christ – to stand up and be counted, unashamed to follow Jesus, no matter the pressures or difficulties that may face them. These words of Jesus continue to this day, as *a sharp two-edged sword* to all who contemplate investing their lives in the pursuit of Jesus. History reveals that many have paid dearly, even with martyrdom, because they were *not ashamed of the gospel of Christ* (Romans 1:16).

The pathway to spiritual maturity is not easy, there are no shortcuts. Believers who want to continue to grow up in Christ will find that many challenges face them and confessing Christ is just one of them. Yet, the difficulties and challenges which we face, present us with the opportunity to make us stronger, more Christlike and mature.

5

The Holy Spirit is God

There are many misconceptions among believers regarding the person and work of the Holy Spirit. Before considering other aspects about him, it must firstly be established that the Holy Spirit is God. Too often we hear him referred to as 'it'. Yes, even by some Christians! It would seem that there is a distinct lack of foundational biblical teaching on the subject of the Holy Spirit.

He is not just some invisible power or force whom God chooses to use (as the Jehovah Witnesses believe), he is God. He is the third member of the Holy Trinity and is equal to the Father and the Son. In Matthew 28:19 when Jesus commissioned the apostles to go and make disciples of all nations, they were to be baptised *in the name of the Father and of the Son and of the Holy Spirit.* In the New Testament, there are several synonymous titles used for the Holy Spirit which help us understand his deity. The following are but a few:

- in Ephesians 2:22 he is referred to as God ... *a dwelling in which God lives by his Spirit*
- in 2 Corinthians 3:18 he is called the Lord ... *which comes from the Lord, who is the Spirit*

- in 2 Timothy 1:14 he is given his own designation
  ... *the Holy Spirit who lives in you*

In the Bible, the Holy Spirit is always viewed as God. In more than 90 places the Spirit of God is referred to as the Holy Spirit. He is neither lesser or greater than the Father and the Son, but equal in every way and distinct as a person. In Psalm 139:7-10, he is omnipresent, being in all places at all times. The prophet Isaiah reminds us that he is omniscient for he knows all things (Isaiah 40:13-14). Then, from Romans 15:19, we understand that he is omnipotent since he has unlimited power.

As we trace the work of the Spirit something is always happening for the Spirit of God is continually active. When we examine his activities they attest his deity. For example, in Genesis 1:2, he is active in creation, *the Spirit of God was hovering over the waters.* Then, in Romans 8:11, he is the giver of eternal life, *he who raised Christ from the dead will also give life to your mortal bodies through his Spirit.* In Matthew 28:19, divine honour is attributed to him. Scripture speaks repeatedly of the Holy Spirit as the Spirit of God and the Spirit of Jesus Christ. The Holy Spirit is ascribed with the attributes of God, is equated with God, and does work that only God can do.

If the Holy Spirit was not a person, then the believer could not experience a personal relationship with Christ. *And if anyone does not have the Spirit of Christ, he does not belong to Christ ... you have received the Spirit of sonship* (Romans 8:9, 15). The bond between us and our Saviour would be reduced to something impersonal and almost abstract if he was not a person. It is not surprising, then, that Paul writes: *So then, just as you received Christ Jesus as Lord, continue to live in him* (Colossians 2:6).

However, because he is a person with all the characteristics of a person, he shares with us the intimacies and purpose of the Father and the Son. It is impossible to overestimate the importance and role of the Holy Spirit in relation to Christian experience, for all that God communicates to us, right from the moment of the new birth, takes place through the operation of the Spirit. He himself is God living in our mortal body, *For he lives with you and will be in you* (John 14:17).

Because he is a person, he has a personality. He speaks, creates, guides, plans, teaches and prays (more about these in later chapters). He has affections, Ephesians 4:30; he makes intercession, John 14:26; he has a will, 1 Corinthians 12:11. If normal Christian living is anything, it is about living a life interacting with, listening to, and knowing the intimate reality of his peace, presence and power. It is to experience his transforming grace, always shaping and changing us into the likeness of Christ. What are we to say to all this? The Apostle John provides the answer: *How great is the love the Father has lavished on us, that we should be called children of God* (1 John 3:1).

As we contemplate the Holy Spirit of God, we call to mind one who was active in the creation of this gloriously majestic universe, which is beyond specific and dimensional understanding. *Can you fathom the mysteries of God? Can you probe the limits of the Almighty? They are higher than the heavens ... They are deeper than the depths of the grave – what can you know?* (Job 11:7-8). *He has made everything beautiful in his time. He also set eternity in the hearts of men; yet they cannot fathom what God has done from beginning to end* (Ecclesiastes 3:11). Scripture reminds us that what God created by his Spirit (Genesis 1:2), he did so out of nothing (Hebrews 11:3). At the word of his command all things came into being; it was not a reshaping of something that already existed, but out of nothing!

The greatness of God is not only witnessed in the wonders of creation, but also in salvation. When God created he spoke words, but to provide a remedy for sin and the redemption of mankind words were not enough. The whole Bible from beginning to end unfolds God's wonderful plan of salvation. His grace, mercy and love are seen on every page, pointing towards the sacrificial gift of his Son. The Old Testament looked towards the cross, whilst the New Testament declared the event itself and explains its unique message.

It is God's purpose that sinners be reconciled to God, thereby entering into a living, eternal relationship with him through his Son; this is only possible through the work of the Holy Spirit. That God should want to take up residence in the lives of ordinary sinful people is quite staggering. Yet he does! All that God has purposed and planned for those who come to faith takes place by his Spirit – he is the one who indwells us, he alone is the vital link between God and man. He informs us about the Father and Son and makes them known to us. Jesus said to his disciples: *All that belongs to the Father is mine. That is why I said the Spirit will take what is mine and make it known to you* (John 16:15).

The relationship between the believer and the Holy Spirit is, essentially, one of intimacy. Because he is a person, he can be hurt and offended. Paul writes: *And do not grieve the Holy Spirit of God, with whom you were sealed for the day of redemption* (Ephesians 4:30). Later we shall consider the implications of this in our daily walk with God. However, for the moment, the important point to remember is that believers do not simply come under the influence of God at conversion (although they do), they become possessed by God through the reception of his Spirit. Believers become the possession of God. Peter writes: *But you are a chosen people, a royal priesthood, a holy nation, a people belonging to God ... Once you were not a people, but now you are the people of God* (1 Peter 2:9-10).

The reception of the Holy Spirit makes us very special people who have been reconciled to God. It makes us more complete and united to God as was his intended purpose. Unless the Holy Spirit was a person, and God, this would have been impossible. John Peck comments: 'If the Spirit were not personal, then his influence upon us would not be personal; it would be in some way alien to us, artificial. It would be more like a drug, or at the best a kind of hypnotic influence. His control of us would make us less than persons.'

Having established the deity of the Holy Spirit from Holy Scripture, it remains for us to consider our response to this glorious relationship we have with God through his Spirit. That the living God has made our bodies his dwelling place, and chosen to unfold his eternal purpose through his Spirit, surely calls for a fitting response.

Paul informs us in 2 Corinthians 3:18 of the Spirit's role in the believers life, when he notes: *And we who with unveiled faces all reflect the Lord's glory, are being transformed into his likeness with ever-increasing glory, which comes from the Lord who is the Spirit.* Our response must surely be that of complete submission to the Spirit. To listen to his voice, heed his promptings, submit to his will, and yield to his every unction is the very least that we can do.

The work of the Holy Spirit in our lives is to bring glory to God and increasingly help us to be more and more like Jesus, in thought, word and deed. To know the reality of the living God at work in our lives is, undoubtedly, our deepest joy and greatest privilege! *Do you not know that you are God's temple and that God's Spirit lives in you* (1 Corinthians 3:16).

6

Life begins
with birth

The beginning of life, as we understand it, commences with physical birth. From the moment a baby is born, a life of growth, development and discovery is expected to follow. In short, without birth there cannot be life! In this respect, the same is true of spiritual birth, of which the Bible has much to teach us. The fact is, a normal Christian life cannot be experienced unless a normal spiritual birth has taken place. The purpose of this chapter is to understand the necessity of spiritual birth and how it takes place.

Spiritual birth is often associated with becoming a Christian. Referring to someone becoming a Christian or being born again is virtually saying the same thing, so long as we understand what these terms mean. It is, therefore, important to recognise what a Christian is not, as many people use the word Christian more with moral implications than spiritual. There is a vast difference between Churchianity and Christianity! Becoming a Christian is not simply deciding to do or believe certain things.

For example:

- Attend church or get involved in church activities
- Read and pray

- Believe that God exists
- Try and change morally and socially
- Be a better person and give to good causes

Although Christians do these things, it is not the act of doing them that makes them a Christian. Before moving on to examine what makes a person a Christian and how spiritual birth takes place, it may prove helpful to identify the only three occasions in the New Testament where the word 'Christian' is used.

Firstly, in Acts 11:26, *The disciples were called Christians first at Antioch.* This title was initially used as a derogatory term, but primarily it referred to those who had taken a conscious decision to turn their back on their old way of life, having repented of their sin, and follow Jesus Christ and his teaching.

Secondly, in Acts 26:28, *Then King Agrippa said to Paul, 'Do you think in such a short time you can persuade me to be a Christian.'* These words came during Paul's defence of the gospel when he was telling Agrippa why and how he had become a Christian.

Thirdly, in 1 Peter 4:16, *If you suffer for being a Christian do not be ashamed.* It was costly to be a Christian, and was a life-changing commitment which called at that time for great courage! Deciding to become a Christian was not taken lightly for it meant persecution.

Perhaps the best way to describe what makes a person a Christian is to use three words, Christ in you. Another way to say the same thing is found in 2 Corinthians 5:17, *If anyone is in Christ he is a new creation; the old has gone, the new has come.* A Christian is a person who has received

Christ into their life by his Spirit. To help us understand the work of the Holy Spirit in relation to spiritual birth we must turn to Scripture. In particular, we turn to the third chapter of John's Gospel where a man called Nicodemus came to speak with Jesus at night. Nicodemus is not mentioned in the first three Gospels, it is John who records his entrance into Holy Scripture. What do we know about this man?

- He was religious. He was both a member of the Jewish ruling council (Sanhedrin) and according to John 3:10, also *a teacher of Israel*. This man was a theologian, dedicated to teaching the law and the tradition of the elders. He was a Jewish religious expert.
- He was respectable. His position in the Sanhedrin and in religious education would have given him high social status. He was a pillar of society.
- He was rich. When Jesus died, Nicodemus brought seventy-five pounds of myrrh and aloes to embalm Jesus' body (John 19:39). Only a wealthy person could have done this.

Jesus underlined the importance of what he was about to say with, *I tell you the truth*. In other words, 'I most solemnly assure you.' In Nicodemus, we have a man who, in the eyes of many, would seem to have everything – religion, respectability, and riches. Yet he was unsatisfied and searching for spiritual fulfilment, hence his visit to speak with Jesus. We have no detail as to the beginning of their conversation.

However, Jesus wasted no time in coming to the main issue. He tells Nicodemus that *no one can enter the kingdom of God unless he is born again* (verse 3). The words *born again* can also be translated as *born from above*, indicating the source of this birth, it is something

God alone can do! Jesus' use of the word *enter* is also a reminder that the human race in its natural sinful state is outside the kingdom of God. Spiritual rebirth is the only means of entering the kingdom. In John 14:6, Jesus said: *I am the way.*

To *see* the kingdom is to 'understand' the kingdom. To understand the kingdom of God a person must be born again, they must be remade by the power of God. This must have sounded like a riddle to Nicodemus. What did this mean to him? Nicodemus heard Jesus' reply, but clearly did not understand (verse 4). He could understand physical birth and enquired how this was possible when he was old ... could this be repeated?

Jesus then got to the crux of the matter. This new birth was not physical, it was spiritual, described in verse 5 as being *born of water and the Spirit.* This point is made in verse 6 where we read: *Flesh gives birth to flesh, but the Spirit gives birth to Spirit.* But what did Jesus mean by *water and the Spirit?* This phrase is to be found nowhere else in the entire New Testament.

Some consider water to be a reference to Christian baptism. The problem with this view is that in Scripture baptism took place following salvation. It was a public witness, a telling forth that a person had come to faith in Christ, that new birth had taken place. Although baptism was important and expected following conversion, it was not essential for salvation.

The likeliest meaning is that water refers to inner purity. Bearing in mind the ministry of John the Baptist and the challenge to *repent,* the requirement of repentance is in keeping with the message of the gospel. Thus, *water and the Spirit* suggests two essentials for new birth i.e. inner cleansing and the reception of the Spirit. Without these no one can enter the kingdom of God. Jesus made it clear that being *born again of the Spirit* was quite distinct from a natural fleshly birth. Natural birth is limited to physical life on earth and will decay with the passing of time and die. Spiritual birth is supernatural and is unending in duration and heavenly in its destination.

Jesus' words in verse 7 were intended to reinforce to Nicodemus the fact that there was no other way, *You must be born again.* The only way to be reconciled to God was through new birth. In verse 8, Jesus used the example of the wind to explain the spiritual nature of this birth. Unlike physical birth which is visible, spiritual birth is invisible. Although the wind cannot be seen, its force and effect can be! The reality of the wind is seen by what it does.

Likewise, the reality of new birth, though invisible, becomes visible through the inner work of the Holy Spirit. New birth begins with the reception of the Spirit, *to all who received him* (John 1:12-13). In 2 Corinthians 3:18, we read: *And we ... are being transformed into his likeness with ever-increasing glory, which comes from the Lord, who is the Spirit.* The evidence that a person is born again is seen in the transformed life.

The Apostle Paul writes: *And if anyone does not have the Spirit of Christ, he does not belong to Christ* (Romans 8:9). In other words, whatever a person is, or is not, whatever they have done or not done, if they have not received the Holy Spirit into their life they do not belong to God. They are not a Christian because the Spirit of Christ does not reside within them.

These verses demonstrate what gross spiritual ignorance there may be in the minds of great and learned men like Nicodemus. Religious knowledge and sincerity do not always equate with truth and spirituality. Such was the case with Nicodemus.

From verse 9 it is clear that he is baffled, *How can this be? Nicodemus asked.* He did not understand the truth of new birth taught by Jesus. Care must be taken, however, not to be harsh with this man. Spiritual blindness may come in many forms; in this case, it was his Pharisaic background and education. It must have been difficult for Nicodemus, this was new and radical teaching! However, Jesus made it very clear that to be right in God's sight, to enter the kingdom of God, there was no other way.

There would come a time when Nicodemus would understand deeper spiritual truths (heavenly things), but on this occasion he found it difficult to believe earthly things (verse 12). To understand *heavenly things*, new birth was a necessity and would require the work of the Holy Spirit. *The man without the Spirit does not accept the things that come from the Spirit of God ... because they are not spiritually discerned* (1 Corinthians 2:14).

The Christian life begins with spiritual birth. From that moment onwards we have the responsibility to submit daily to the Holy Spirit. Only through such an act can we ever experience the reality of normal Christian living and live the life which God intended for us. The world around us needs to see the real thing, the Christian life lived in the full power of the Holy Spirit. The world needs to witness what God can do with those spiritually born again and completely surrendered to him. Only then will the normal Christian life be in evidence! *In his great mercy he has given us new birth* (1 Peter 1:3). A life worth living begins with the spiritual birth.

7

Filled with the Spirit

We discovered in the previous chapter that conversion takes place when the Holy Spirit is received into the believer's life. From that moment onward a work of God's grace begins, changing and transforming, glorifying God and exalting his Son, bringing about the visible life of Christ in the human frame. It is impossible to over-value the necessity of the Spirit's indwelling and his work, accomplishing the purpose of God through his people. In every age the Holy Spirit is indispensable to the life and health of the church.

On 31 August 1857, C H Spurgeon uttered the following words, suitable and relevant for all ages: 'The grand thing the church wants in this time is God's Holy Spirit. You all get up plans and say, "Now if the church were altered a little bit, it would go on better." You think that if there were different ministers, or different church order, or something different, then all would be well. No, dear friends, it is not there that the mistake lies; it is that we want more of the Spirit ... that is the church's great want, and until that want be supplied, we may reform and reform, and still be just the same. All we want is the Spirit of God.'

The importance of the work of the Spirit is made clear by the command: *Be filled with the Spirit* (Ephesians 5:18). Within the context of this passage, we discover that being filled with the Spirit will determine how we live, worship and behave. It is imperative that believers understand what it means to be filled with the Spirit and how it is to be obtained. To live as God intended and be normal Christians, we must know and experience the reality of being *filled with the Spirit* – the Christian's birthright.

It is vital to our understanding to remember that the Holy Spirit is a person, and that new birth (conversion) takes place following repentance, faith in Jesus Christ and the receiving of the Holy Spirit. This means that it is a person, the Holy Spirit of God, who takes up residence in the believer's life. As a result, they become children of God, for we read: *Yet to all who received him, to those who believed in his name, he gave them the right to become children of God* (John 1:12).

We must remember not to refer to the Holy Spirit as 'it' or just some 'influence, power or force' that we receive, he is the third person of the Trinity. Unless we grasp this truth at the outset, our understanding of what it means to be filled with the Spirit and our relationship with him will be impaired and lead us into confusion.

In Ephesians 5:15-17, the Apostle Paul prepares his readers for the command to be filled with the Spirit (verse 18), by stressing two things:

Firstly, *Be very careful, then, how you live.* The believer's life and lifestyle must be one that is empowered and directed by the Holy Spirit. To live outwith his influence and depend upon self is, according to verse 15, *unwise.* This is not a basis for normal Christian living or the mark of one born anew of the Spirit. Christians must display in their lives a wisdom that is from God.

Secondly, Paul writes: *Do not be foolish, but understand what the Lord's will is.* How is a Christian to understand the will of God? By listening to and obeying the Holy Spirit. No Christian can fulfil God's will for their life apart from being filled with his Spirit. The alternative is to live a life that is self-centred and self-directed and end up glorifying self. This is both unwise and foolish, says Paul.

In verse 18, we have the command to *be filled with the Spirit.* The Greek word for *be filled* is 'pleroo' and is, literally, translated, 'be being kept filled'. This means, continue to be filled, keep on being filled. Being filled with the Spirit is not an option for believers, but a divine mandate. Why should this be a command? Because it is not possible for the believer to live a holy, God-glorifying life, discovering the wonders of his will, unless the Spirit has complete control.

As children of God, we are his subjects called to live under his reign and authority. His rule in our lives, therefore, takes place through the work of the Holy Spirit. Having received the Holy Spirit as a complete person, how are we to understand the command to continually be filled with him? Surely he is either in our lives or not! If he is already in our lives, how can we have more of him? After all, it is not possible to receive 'part' of a person. One answer to this is although we cannot have more of him, he can have more of us! The following explanation will help us understand:

It is sad to see many Christians living today far below the level of what God intended for them. They have lost their sense of joy, victory and purpose in their relationship with God. Too often the Spirit-filled Christian is looked on as something of a super saint, instead of someone who is normal. John MacArthur comments: 'Although every Christian is indwelt, baptised, and sealed by the Spirit, unless he is also filled with the Spirit, he will live in spiritual weakness, retardation, frustration and defeat.' The challenge of the day for all who confess Christ as Lord and Saviour is that of being filled with the Spirit.

How can we be filled with the Holy Spirit? In short ... complete submission to him! But what does this mean, what are the practicalities, what are we to do? In 1 Corinthians 6:19, we read: *Do you not know that your body is a temple of the Holy Spirit, who is in you, whom you have received from God? You are not your own; you were bought with a price. Therefore honour God with your body.*

Believers belong to God and are his temple, a place of worship where God lives by his Spirit; he lives within us. What a joy! What a privilege! Yes, but what a responsibility! Temples must be kept clean. There must be inner cleansing. There can be no room for unconfessed sin in our lives. Sin will always be a barrier to our relationship with God and will hinder the work of the Spirit. We must continually come clean! Every sinful thought or deed will block the Spirit's flow.

When I was a young boy, in the town where I lived there was a well known meeting place. It was a beautiful fountain situated in the centre of a tree-lined avenue just outside the town's main library. It was built of fine stone and marble and was meant to function as a fountain, providing clear fresh water for those who were thirsty.

Unfortunately, what I remember most about this fountain was that water rarely, if ever, flowed from it. It did not fulfil its intended purpose! Why?

The answer is simple. The water pipe leading to the fountain was in good condition and fresh water was there in abundance but it would not flow through the fountain because it was blocked. Pieces of gravel, dirt, stones, all sorts of rubbish (even weeds) were blocking the water's flow. It was not a clean fountain! The message is clear. Only when the fountain was cleaned out would the water flow and once again shoot high into the air, thereby fulfilling its intended purpose. There was no shortage of water – just too much dirt!

Likewise, in the believer's life, the sin that blocks the Spirit's flow must be confessed. When this happens the Holy Spirit will flood our lives to overflowing. It takes very little to hinder his flow. A few small stones could block the fountain. In the same way, it takes just a few sinful thoughts or deeds, just a little pride or ego, just a little of anything from our sinful nature that is allowed to go unchecked will cause a blockage, it doesn't take much! That is why Paul writes: *Put to death, therefore, whatever belongs to your earthly nature* (Colossians 3:5).

It is in this sense that he can have more of us. Unless we are empty of self, we cannot be filled. We must never flirt with sinful thoughts or deeds if we are to be filled with the Spirit. We must learn never to tinker or compromise with any form of sin. No! Sin must be put to death. This is what Paul meant when he said: *I have been crucified with Christ and I no longer live but Christ lives in me* (Galatians 2:20).

If the first prerequisite for the infilling of the Spirit is confession and inner cleansing, there is yet another condition. There must be the desire to be filled, we must want it. There must be a heartfelt hunger that wants to be filled with the fulness of God more than anything else. We must want his power, presence and will before all else. We must also have a right motive.

Our goal must be for the greater glory of God. There must be submission to the Spirit, a yielding which allows him to have his way completely; breaking, moulding and reshaping us into the likeness of Jesus. The willingness to die to self is vital. We must be in a position where we want only what God wants. There is no easy way to grow in spiritual maturity, there are no shortcuts to being filled with the Spirit. Every day is a new day of confession and submission, inviting the Spirit to fill us anew.

A W Tozer writes: 'This desire to be filled must become all absorbing in your life. If there is anything in your life bigger than your desire to be a Spirit-filled Christian, you will never be a Spirit-filled Christian until that is cured. If there is anything in your life more demanding than your longing after God, then you will never be a Spirit-filled Christian.'

The first part of Ephesians 5:18 reads: *Do not get drunk on wine, which leads to debauchery.* Here we have a contrast between wine and the Spirit. How can we tell if someone is full of wine or some other strong drink? We can easily detect it because of the way they talk. Usually they are incoherent and slurred in their speech. The way in which they walk is also noticeable. They have difficulty going in the right direction, or even keeping upright. Furthermore, their breath smells of drink, they cannot hide the fact that they have been drinking. In short, they are under the influence and effect of alcohol.

Here are the lessons: when a believer is full of the Spirit it will be noticeable by the way they walk. Their life will be under the direction of the Spirit, orderly and purposeful, and full of integrity. Then their speech will be seasoned with grace, under the control of the Spirit in all that is said, thereby, graciously commending the Saviour. In contrast to the smell of drink, Paul writes: *But thanks be to God, who always leads us in triumphal procession in Christ and through us spreads everywhere the fragrance of the knowledge of him. For we are the aroma of Christ.* Here is the scent that makes Christ almost tangible in the believer's life, detectable by others – a Christlike aroma.

In verses 19-21 we discover the results of being filled with the Spirit. There will be a spirit of praise and worship, singing and giving thanks to God the Father for *everything*, not just in some things, but in everything. When our relationship with the Lord is right, he becomes the sole object of our worship and, furthermore, the believer's relationship with each other should also be God-glorifying, for we read: *Submit to one another out of reverence for Christ.* Being filled with the Spirit, then, affects every aspect of life, including our relationship with God and one another.

In conclusion, having given thought to the necessity of being filled with the Spirit and what the criterion is for this to happen, there is something else to remember. The Holy Spirit cannot be chained or restricted in any way that he does not want. He is God and, in every sense, will do what he wants, where he wants, and in the manner he chooses. There are times when he will choose to anoint individuals or pour out his Spirit on larger gatherings for his chosen purpose. But he will do so in accordance with his own character and always for the glory of God.

In Luke 2:25-32 we have an example of this. A devout Old Testament believer called Simeon was looking and waiting for the coming Messiah. Simeon held the child Jesus in his arms, praised God for him and blessed his parents, recognising that in Jesus the promised Messiah had come. In this connection we read that the Holy Spirit was *upon* Simeon (verse 25). The Holy Spirit *revealed* to him that he would not die until he had seen Christ (verse 26) and that he was *moved* (or led) by the Spirit to go into the temple (verse 27).

In the Old Testament period the Spirit of God often came upon people for God's intended purpose. Following the giving out of the Spirit at Pentecost in Acts 2, the Holy Spirit indwelt those who came to faith: *Do you not know that your body is a temple of the Holy Spirit, who is in you, whom you have received from God* (1 Corinthians 6:19). This is a blessing beyond which Old Testament believers ever experienced.

At times God will pour out his Spirit in ways both unexpected and undeserved. We cannot package or pigeonhole the Holy Spirit or predict his operations. He is God the Holy Spirit and will act in ways that, at times, are mysterious to our understanding. Being filled with the Spirit is a privilege too great for words to express and is a must for all who seek to live a normal Christian life.

8
Walking in the Spirit

Those who claim to know Jesus Christ must bear this truth out in their everyday lives. The Apostle John writes: *This is how we know we are in him: Whoever claims to live in him must walk as Jesus did* (1 John 2:6). Jesus is the perfect role model. From the outset of our Christian experience the challenge is to follow Christ: *If anyone will come after me, he must deny himself and take up his cross and follow me* (Mark 8:34).

Essentially, our link with Jesus is relational, for through faith in him we have become children of God and, as such, have a responsibility to bear the family resemblance. Therefore, we must walk as Jesus did! But how did Jesus walk? He walked as one anointed by the Holy Spirit (Matthew 3:16), in perfect unity and fellowship with his Father and in accordance with his will (John 17:21). He preached the truth, lived out the truth and brought glory to God through all that he said and did (John 17:4). His life was one of glorifying God and blessing others.

To walk in the Spirit is to walk with a sense of God's purpose, filled with the Spirit, hearing his voice and obeying his every word.

How then can we walk in this way? Is it really possible? Yes! But only by submitting to the Holy Spirit!

Walking is what we do to get from one place to another and usually means that we have a destination in mind when we set out. The great thing about being a Christian is that our lives come under the direction of God, no longer should we be a law unto ourselves and live according to what we decide. Our new walk comes under the direction of the Holy Spirit for it is he who leads and guides us according to the Father's will for us. This does not mean that we abandon our common sense or wisdom; on the contrary, we surrender these to the Holy Spirit. In what ways does the Holy Spirit interact with us in our daily walk? What are the criteria to walking in the Spirit?

(a) Led by the Spirit

In Romans 8:2 we read of two laws, the law of sin and the law of the Spirit of life. The law of sin points to the sinful nature. It means being under the influence of the old sinful nature, bringing us under its control. Submission to this law can only bring defeat and failure, leading us away from the purpose and presence of God to a life of self-pleasure and self-glory. This pathway leads in the wrong direction and stands in opposition to discovering the great blessings of 'normal' Christian living.

But there is another law: *Therefore, there is no condemnation for those who are in Christ Jesus, because through Christ Jesus the law of the Spirit of life set me free from the law of sin and death* (Romans 8:1). Through faith in Christ we have been set free and are to live under this new law, the law of the Spirit, under the influence and control of the

Holy Spirit. We need no longer be held prisoner by the power of sin because the Holy Spirit has set us free. Says Paul: *You, however, are not controlled by the sinful nature but by the Spirit* (Romans 8:9).

This new law calls for our submission to the Spirit. We must be willing to be led by the Spirit, inviting and allowing him to direct all our affairs. According to Paul: *those who are led by the Spirit are sons of God* (Romans 8:14). Being led by the Spirit is evidence that we are sons and daughters of God. This wonderful, distinctive feature ought to mark out those who claim to be Christians, living their lives under the direction of the Spirit of God.

In Galatians 5:16 the Apostle Paul introduces a wider picture by using the word *live ... So I say, live by the Spirit, and you will not gratify the desires of the sinful nature.* Essentially, the Christian life is one of conflict and warfare, a battle of two natures! John Stott writes: 'As we learn to walk in the Spirit, the flesh becomes increasingly subdued. But the flesh and the Spirit remain, and the conflict between them is fierce and unremitting.' How then are we to triumph over the sinful nature with all its influence, wrong thoughts and temptations? Paul says: *live by the Spirit.*

The concept of living by the Spirit, I suggest, embraces more than just being led. It is a reference to every aspect of daily life. It calls for the believer to depend on the Spirit in all things, considering nothing too small or insignificant for the Spirit's interest or help. After all, he is God the Holy Spirit and is *familiar with all our ways* (Psalm 139:3). Being filled with and walking in the Spirit involves our day to day and moment by moment submission to the Spirit's control.

(b) Sensitivity of the Spirit

Having received the Holy Spirit at our spiritual birth, he will never leave us; we cannot lose our salvation because of our sins, weaknesses or failures. However, it is possible to lose our joy and the fulness of the Spirit's blessing. It is possible for believers to live as though the Spirit was absent; when this happens (and it can) it is a tragedy!

This is possible when we grieve the Spirit. Paul writes: *And do not grieve the Holy Spirit of God, with whom you were sealed for the day of redemption* (Ephesians 4:30). The Greek word for *grieved* is 'lupeo' and means 'to cause pain or distress'. Because the Holy Spirit is a person, he is sensitive with feelings and emotions; he can be offended and hurt.

Very often the source of breakdown in human relationships is caused by insensitivity to others. This can be true within a marriage. Although living with each other under the same roof, a couple may only be going through the motions of a normal marriage, having lost any joy or sense of purpose in their relationship, so that it is a marriage in name only.

Likewise, Christians are in danger of becoming insensitive to the Spirit and stop listening to his voice. Whatever violates the will of God and the purity of the heart will grieve the Holy Spirit. This in turn may lead to subduing the work of the Spirit, thereby forfeiting his power and blessings. God forbid that we should ever turn our backs on the Spirit. Paul's warning is clear: *Do not put out the Spirit's fire* (1 Thessalonians 5:19).

John MacArthur comments: 'How can we do that which is so

displeasing to the one by whom [we] have been sealed for the day of redemption? The Holy Spirit is God's personal mark of authenticity on us, his stamp of divine approval. How can we grieve the one who is our Helper, Comforter, Teacher, Advocate, Divine Resident of our hearts, and guarantor of our eternal redemption? How can we ungraciously grieve God's infinitely gracious Holy Spirit? He has done so much for us that, out of gratitude, we ought not to grieve him.'

All that the believer has comes from Christ by his Spirit, he is our lifeline with the Father and is the instrument of our eternal union with him. Having become children of God and adopted into his family, all heavenly communications come to us through the Spirit. To be sensitive to the Spirit is not only our privilege, but also our deepest obligation, if we are to live normal Christian lives which reflect the glory of God.

In Galatians 5:25, we read: *Since we live by the Sprit, let us keep in step with the Spirit.* That means we heed his every prompting and obey his will, taking our direction in life from him. As previously mentioned, this is evidence that we are children of God. Keeping in step with the Spirit also introduces the thought of progress and unity, advancing one stride at a time towards complete consecration to the Lord. The picture of walking one step at a time is good and helpful because in our continual battle against the old nature, victory is to be achieved in this way ... one step at a time!

A simple thought may prove helpful in our understanding of being led by the Spirit and walking in the Spirit. Being led by the Spirit is something the Spirit does, whilst walking in the Spirit is something we are actively called to do. Unless we are led by the Spirit, we are unlikely to walk in the right direction. Being sensitive to the Spirit is essential if we are to *keep in step with him.*

(c) Taught by the Spirit

To many people the Bible may seem an interesting, yet lifeless book ... one difficult to understand. Some parts can be followed like any other book; a person can increase their knowledge of the Bible by reading and studying it. However, unless we have help outwith ourselves, we shall never understand it. This is one of the responsibilities of the Holy Spirit.

In John 14:26, Jesus said to his disciples: *But the Counsellor, the Holy Spirit, whom the Father will send in my name, will teach you all things and will remind you of everything I have said to you.* As we read the Bible the Holy Spirit will bring understanding to us of truths and things that the natural (sinful) mind cannot understand.

It is the special duty of the Holy Spirit to apply truth to the hearts of all believers so that when he speaks into our lives we will recognise that what he says is true. In John 14:17 Jesus referred to him as *the Spirit of truth.* Being the truth in person, he guides his people into the realm of truth which is found in Christ and his redemption. He is the interpreter of the Father's purpose for our daily lives, bringing understanding to our hearts and minds.

Do we want to know right from wrong, truth from error? Then we must listen to the Spirit of truth! His communication to us is singularly unique for only those who have come to faith in Christ will understand what he is saying. In contrast, the non-Christian cannot discern him because he does not know him: *The world cannot accept him, because it neither sees him nor knows him* (verse 17). Many believers testify to the fact that only following their conversion did they begin to understand the Scriptures.

The work of the Holy Spirit also has a vital role with regard to the world, for we read: *When he comes, he will convict the world of guilt in regard to sin and righteousness and judgment* (John 16:8). In that respect, his ministry is that of bringing an awareness of sin, revealing to men and women that they have sinned and by nature are in an unrighteous state before God. Looking back to their pre-Christian condition, many believers can recall their inner emptiness and spiritually unfulfilled state. This is often described as a preparative work of the Holy Spirit before conversion.

Perhaps the most noble and deeply profound ministry of the Holy Spirit is found in John 16:14, where Jesus says: *He will bring glory to me by taking from what is mine and making it known to you.* How glorious is this? That the Spirit will teach us and help us understand the things concerning Christ is, for the believer, the blessing of all blessings!

The Spirit of truth will reveal to us the person of Christ in ever-increasing measure. Day by day, moment by moment, as we keep in step with the Spirit, he will unfold before us the beauty and glory of Jesus.

William Hendriksen writes: 'He will cause the virtues of Christ to be proclaimed, showing forth his power, holiness, love, etc., and causing these to become resplendently manifest among the nations. He will take that which is Christ's – the very substance of his teaching regarding the purpose of redemption, manner of salvation, etc. – and will enlarge it. Whatever Christ has done, is doing, will do (for the Church) is the theme of the Holy Spirit's teaching.'

In conclusion: We live in a world that needs to witness the life of Christ, hear his words and see the power of a transformed life in his children. We have a divine mandate to bear the resemblance of our Saviour: *And we, who with unveiled faces all reflect the Lord's glory, are being transformed into his likeness with ever-increasing glory, which comes from the Lord, who is the Spirit* (2 Corinthians 3:18). If we are to walk in the Spirit then we must be led by the Spirit, sensitive to the Spirit, and taught by the Spirit. This is the recipe for the transformed life!

The world around us is confused; as Christians, we must do more than verbalise our faith, our daily lives must embody what we believe. Men and women want to see reality, not just hear words without substance. If we are telling others that in Christ there is life worth living, then we must live such a life! Charles Swindoll's comments are most relevant: 'Superficiality is the curse of our age. The doctrine of instant satisfaction is a primary spiritual problem. The deeper life is a subject greatly admired but rarely experienced – we sing of its virtues, but don't embrace them.'

There are no shortcuts to spiritual maturity; the deeper life is costly, it does not come without price and is only to be found in the company of Jesus Christ and our complete surrender to the Spirit.

9

Empowered by
the Spirit

For three years the disciples followed Jesus, listened to his gracious words and witnessed his miraculous powers. During that period they learned much about the Lord and his teaching, yet they were still very vulnerable and weak men. At times our Lord was disappointed at their lack of faith and understanding, rebuking them accordingly: *You of little faith ... do you still not understand?* (Matthew 16:8-9).

Most of them were not there when Jesus needed them most, at the cross! Yet, following the outpouring of the Holy Spirit at Pentecost these same men were transformed, never to be the same again. They would be empowered by the Holy Spirit to become witnesses to the gospel of Christ and experience the reality of the transformed life (Acts 1:8).

Jesus had appeared many times during the forty days following his resurrection. We read: *On one of these occasions, while he was eating with them, he gave them this command: 'Do not leave Jerusalem, but wait for the gift my Father promised, which you have heard me speak about. For John baptised with water but in a few days you will be baptised with the Holy Spirit.'* (Acts 1:4). Jesus commanded them to wait for this special manifestation. In the first three Gospels the same prophecy was made to John the Baptist (cf. Matthew 3:11; Mark 1:8; Luke 3:16).

In the Old Testament, Isaiah and Joel prophesied this. What they were to experience was not by chance, nor was it the result of anything they had done. It wasn't even the result of them being constantly in prayer. This was the chosen time by God to send the Holy Spirit following our Lord's ascension into heaven.

Those gathered in this upper room were all believers (about 120 of them) and they were waiting for the Spirit. They heard the blowing of a strong wind and saw what seemed to be tongues of fire rest upon them (both wind and fire are symbols of the Spirit and the Word). In Ezekiel 37 the breath of life is seen entering the dead bodies as a wind blowing upon them and bringing them to life. In John 3 Jesus used the wind to illustrate the nature of conversion.

In Acts 2:4, we read: *All of them were filled with the Holy Spirit.* This was their baptism in the Holy Spirit. In John 14:17 Jesus promised them that he would not leave them as orphans, *for he lives with you and will be in you.* This was a most wonderful and unique moment in history. The Holy Spirit had now been given and would take up residence in their lives. Their bodies were now the temple of the Holy Spirit. Such would be the case from that time onwards for all who would trust in Christ for salvation.

There would only be one Pentecost, just as there was only one Calvary, one empty tomb, one resurrection, and one ascension. The coming of the Holy Spirit was to inaugurate a new relationship between God and mankind. The astonishing beginning and the remarkable growth rate of the New Testament church, as recorded in Acts, can only be explained by the outpouring of the Holy Spirit as promised by Jesus.

Any endeavour or act of service carried out in the name of Christ must be done in the power of the Spirit, otherwise it will be a fleshly enterprise which is likely to be more self-exalting than Christ-glorifying. The resources to live for Christ and serve his kingdom come from the Spirit. God's work can only be done in God's power!

Suffering defeat is the all too common experience of believers as they seek to live for Christ and his kingdom. From the moment of conversion we enter into a battleground, not a playground, not a life of ease, but a life of possessing and entering into all that God has planned for us.

In the Old Testament the land promised to Israel by God had to be possessed. Israel did not simply march in, set up their homes and build their cities. No! They had to fight and overpower the enemy. Battles had to be fought before victories could be won. There were times when Israel suffered defeat and failure. Generally speaking, these were times when Israel trusted in her own strength. The spirit of independence is badly flawed for it only leads to defeat. Joshua and the Israelites faced mountainous tasks and obstacles, yet they were promised victory only on the basis of God's power. They had to learn to trust in the Lord.

Likewise, believers, in the pursuit of holy living and a God-glorifying way of life need the help of the Holy Spirit; he is the key, the source of power. Spiritual warfare demands spiritual resources. Because the Spirit lives within us we have the power to overcome. In 2 Corinthians 4, Paul shared the pressures he faced and how he got through them: *We are hard pressed on every side, but not crushed; perplexed, but not in despair; persecuted, but not abandoned; struck down, but not destroyed* (verse 8).

How was he able to overcome? How did he make it through such circumstances? His answer is found in these words: *But we have this treasure in jars of clay to show that this all-surpassing power is from God and not from us* (verse 7). We may never face situations as dark and difficult as Paul, but the principles are the same – to fight our battles, whatever they may be, we need the power of the Spirit. Notice the words: *and not from us.*

In Philippians 4:13 Paul makes it clear where his strength came from: *I can do everything through him who gives me strength.* Then, as part of his prayer for the church at Ephesus, he writes: *I pray that out of his glorious riches he may strengthen you with power through his Spirit in your inner being ... he is able to do immeasurably more than all we ask or imagine, according to his power that is at work in us* (Ephesians 3:16ff). What gloriously encouraging words!

When David stood before Goliath he faced a foe bigger and stronger than himself. The threat of this nine-foot giant had driven fear into all Israel, so that not even Israel's bravest soldiers would dare to stand before Goliath, *Saul and all the Israelites were dismayed and terrified ... they all ran from him in great fear* (1 Samuel 17:11ff).

This was a battle between good and evil, light and darkness, flesh and Spirit, between the people of God and the ungodly. David was mocked by his brothers and taunted by the enemy. Even King Saul reluctantly allowed David to go and face Goliath ... how pathetic! Yet this typified the spiritual state of Israel at that time.

Before David went to confront Goliath, Saul offered him his armour but David declined. Apart from the armour being too large, there was a more important reason. David said to Goliath: *I come against you in the name of the Lord Almighty* (verse 45). David would not depend upon physical resources (the flesh), but face his enemy in the name (or power) of the Lord Almighty. *It is not by the sword or the spear ... for the battle is the Lord's* (verse 47).

Everything about David was small – his stature, his sling, his staff, and experience. Everything, except his God! God delights to use smallness. We can be too big for God to use, but never too small. David's victory rested on the power of God; against impossible odds, he triumphed. There is also another reason for his success as his motive was for the glory of God, not self-exaltation, so we read: *and the whole world will know that there is a God in Israel* (verse 46).

Beginning at Judges 6 we have the story of Gideon. During a period when Israel were rebellious and insensitive to God's purpose and, as a result, suffered continual defeat, God called Gideon to champion the Israelite cause. At that time Gideon was in a cave beating out wheat for fear of the Midianites when God spoke to him. In Judges 6:12 an angel of the Lord spoke to Gideon, saying: *The Lord is with you, mighty warrior.* At that time he was not a mighty warrior, but that is what he would become!

In response, Gideon declared his own personal weakness and that of his clan (verse 15). The turning point for Gideon came when the Lord said: *I will be with you* (verse 16). As the story unfolds, Gideon's military resources were reduced from 32,000 to 300 by God to show that any victory could only be attributed to the power of God.

Following great success on the battlefield the Israelites wanted Gideon to rule over them (Judges 8:22), but he refused, saying: *The Lord will rule over you* (verse 23). The victory was achieved by the power of God, not Gideon or his resources. Here we have yet another example of how God could turn Israel's failure and defeat into victory and for his glory. By submitting to God's will, Gideon discovered the awesome power of God. His own smallness provided God with the opportunity to perform the miraculous.

It is possible to look on incidents and experiences in the lives of others such as David, and think: 'Well, it's alright for them ... important people, big situations, but what about me? What about God's power in my life? How can I know his power in my every day life?' The wonderful thing about having a personal relationship with God is this, David's God is our God! The power of God in David's life is the same power that is available to all God's children, neither less nor inferior! The same God and the same power!

Should we find it difficult or almost impossible, for example, to share our faith with others, discipline or prioritise our lives, overcome unhelpful habits, get rid of recurring sins or deal with pride or ego, or whatever, then the Holy Spirit can help us. He wants to! We cannot live the transformed and victorious life that exalts Christ unless we daily submit to the Holy Spirit, declaring our weakness and our need of his power. Paul writes: *My grace is sufficient for you, for my power is made perfect in weakness ... I delight in weaknesses ... for when I am weak, then I am strong* (2 Corinthians 12:9ff).

The principles found in the experiences of David and Gideon serve as a teacher and encouragement to us all. They could not face the enemy in their own strength; Peter and the other apostles could not preach or witness to the gospel of Christ in their own strength. Likewise, you and I cannot live for Christ and his kingdom in a God-glorifying way, unless it is in his power.

10
Transformed by the Spirit

'Jesus, you are changing me, by your Spirit you're making me like you; Jesus, you're transforming me, that your loveliness may be seen in all I do. You are the potter and I am the clay; help me to be willing to let you have your way; Jesus, you are changing me as I let you reign supreme within my heart' ... these words, penned by Marilyn Baker, are a wonderful reminder of God's purpose for us and also present us with the challenge of Christ's sovereignty in our lives.

Beginning with new birth, the transforming work of God in our lives takes place through the operation of his Spirit, ever-changing, reshaping and moulding us into the likeness of his Son, Jesus. That this is even possible is a miracle of God's grace and electing love. For sinners to be saved by God's grace is one thing, but to envisage that the work of salvation can actually lead to our continual transformation, and to such an extent that Christ may become visible through us, is quite staggering. G B Duncan comments: 'One of the miracles of the grace of God is what he is able to do with the torn nets of lives surrendered to him.'

It is this theme that Paul has in mind in 2 Corinthians 3:18, where he says: *And we, who with unveiled faces all reflect the Lord's glory, are being transformed into his likeness with ever-increasing glory, which comes from the Lord, who is the Spirit.* The work of Christ is something that was done for us on the cross, but there is another work – the work of Christ in us. This is a work of the Holy Spirit interacting with our will and calling for our obedience and surrender to his purpose. The goal of this work is aimed at bringing glory to the Lord.

Christians are called to reflect the Lord's glory. According to Ephesians 1:12, believers are to live *for the praise of his glory.* We have been created for this very reason. Here in 2 Corinthians 3:7-8, Paul refers to the fading (outward) glory of Moses, contrasting it with the superior ministry of the Spirit which will *be even more glorious,* and in verse 18, *with ever-increasing glory.* This is a glorious work because it reveals and exalts the life of Christ within our mortal bodies. Hence Paul's comment: *So that his life may be revealed in our mortal body* (2 Corinthians 4:11).

The work of transformation, of reshaping and moulding us into the image of our Lord, is essentially one of cooperation between ourselves and the Spirit. In this respect, there are certain key areas to be considered:

Firstly, the transforming of the mind. We read: *Do not conform any longer to the pattern of this world, but be transformed by the renewing of your mind* (Romans 12:2). It is in view of God's mercy and the self-giving of Christ that Paul now makes this appeal to Christian believers. In light of all that God has done for us, the very least we can do is surrender every fibre of our being to the Lord. The work of transforming and renewing by the Spirit begins in the mind.

It is not unreasonable to suggest that the greatest battlefield for the Christian is the mind, the place of decisions. It is here that we formulate our plans and take our decisions; in short, make up our mind before moving into action! Intellect and emotions are involved in this fray as the Holy Spirit vies for the submission of our will.

The direction of our lives is determined by the decisions we have taken in the mind. It is the work of the Spirit to transform our mind thereby bringing us into conformity, not according to the pattern of this world, but with the will of God.

The world wants to control our mind but the Spirit wants to transform it. The Greek word used here for *transform* is 'metamorphosis' and it is used to describe a 'change from within', an inner change which manifests itself in outward behaviour. The same word is used in Matthew 17:2 for the transfiguration of our Lord, where his physical appearance changed as a result of his inward communion with his Father. Warren W Wiersbe comments: 'If the world controls your thinking, you are a conformer; if God controls your thinking, you are a transformer.' How we think determines how we behave.

In Colossians 3, we see this principle at work. In verse 2, we read: *Set your minds on things above, not on earthly things.* Paul begins with the mind because it is the mind that regulates all our thoughts. The mind is the launching pad for all our actions. The practical outworking of this comes in verse 5, where Paul writes: *Put to death, therefore, what belongs to your earthly nature.*

Being transformed by the Spirit commences with the surrendering of our mind, so that our Lord begins our lifetime of continual change with how we think. In effect, this means we are called to submit our will to God's will. This is clear from Romans 12:2, ... *but be transformed by the renewing of your mind. Then you will be able to test and approve what God's will is – his good, pleasing and perfect will.* God's will is good for us, it is the perfect choice!

Secondly, there is the transference of ownership. As believers, we do not belong to ourselves nor can we be a law unto ourselves for we are not our own. Writing in 1 Corinthians 6:19, Paul says: *Do you not know that your body is a temple of the Holy Spirit, who is in you, whom you have received from God? You are not your own; you were bought with a price. Therefore honour God with your body.*

Christians belong to the Lord Jesus, he has bought them. He paid for them with his own blood shed on the cross. Our bodies are referred to as a *temple* in which the Lord has taken up residence by his Spirit (with one supreme purpose, to glorify God). We are indwelt by the Spirit of God. He lives in us, never to leave or forsake us for *no one can snatch them out of my Father's hand* (John 10:30).

Paul writes in Ephesians 1:13 that we were *marked in him with a seal, the promised Holy Spirit, who is a deposit guaranteeing our inheritance.* It is not that the Holy Spirit seals us, but that he is the seal by which we are marked out as belonging to Christ. It is not by being branded on our forehead or by something similar that we belong to Christ, but by having the Holy Spirit indwell us. Just as Christ has bought us with his blood, and as a farmer would brand the sheep he has bought, Christ marks us out by the transforming work of the Spirit. It is the work of the Spirit to make visible the life of Christ.

That believers belong to Christ is put so distinctly and with great clarity by the Apostle Peter: *Once you were not a people, but now you are the people of God; once you had not received mercy, but now you have received mercy* (1 Peter 2:10). Being the people of God is the greatest privilege ever afforded to men and women. Such privilege calls for a fitting response. With the Spirit's help this surely means declaring Christ to be sovereign in our lives. Peter writes: *In your hearts set apart Christ as Lord* (1 Peter 3:15).

This is one of the most demanding challenges that Christians must face for it calls for our complete allegiance to Christ in every department of our lives. The words *set apart* describe the unique position that Christ must occupy in our lives ... he must have no rival or equal and he must have first place in all things. He must be Lord of all or he is not Lord at all! Christ must be on the throne of our hearts! He must reign! In Colossians 1:18, Paul puts it this way: ... *so that in everything he might have the supremacy.* The normal Christian life can only be experienced when Christ is Lord of all and, as an act of the will, believers transfer ownership of all that they are and have to him.

Thirdly, the transforming work of the Spirit calls for our consecration. To consecrate is to set apart for holy use. We have been chosen and set apart by Christ to live for his praise and glory. The first requirement in this respect is the need for self-examination and cleansing. As a temple of the Holy Spirit we must keep the temple clean, no sin must go unconfessed. Sin separates and impairs our fellowship with God. When and where there is unforgiven sin, true intimacy with our Lord cannot be experienced; nothing must go unchecked. We must ask the Holy Spirit to sift us as wheat, revealing anything that may be lurking in any crevice within the heart and mind that requires confession. In this connection, Paul offers excellent advice: *Let us purify ourselves from everything that contaminates body and spirit, perfecting holiness out of reverence for God* (2 Corinthians 7:1). Cleansing precedes consecration.

David writes: *Search me, O God, and know my heart; test me and know my anxious thoughts. See if there is any offensive way in me, and lead me in the way everlasting* (Psalm 139:22-24). Again, in Psalm 51:2-3, following his adultery with Bathsheba, he says: *Wash away all my iniquity and cleanse me from my sin. For I know my transgressions, and my sin is always before me.* Before David could consecrate himself to God, he had to confess his sin and seek cleansing and forgiveness. The prophet Habakkuk writes concerning God's attitude towards sin: *Your eyes are too pure to look on evil; you cannot tolerate wrong* (1:13). The Psalmist makes the point clearly: *If I had cherished sin in my heart, the Lord would not have listened* (Psalm 66:18).

Even the most devout believer may discover at times that they are holding on to some little thing that has not been surrendered to God. Little things can cause big blockages! Rev John MacNeil, in his book, *The Spirit Filled Life*, illustrates this point with a simple story:

'A little child was one day playing with a very valuable vase, when he put his hand into it and could not withdraw it. His father, too, tried his best to get it out, but all in vain. They were talking of breaking the vase, when the father said: "Now, my son, make one more try; open your hand and hold out your fingers straight, as you see me doing, and then pull." To their astonishment the little fellow said: "Oh no, pa, I couldn't put out my fingers like that, for if I did, I would drop my penny." He had been holding on to a penny all the time! How many of us are like him! Drop the copper, surrender, let go, and God will give you gold.'

And so, if we are to know the Spirit-filled life, and to submit to the transforming power of the Spirit, we must see ourselves as we really are, as God sees us, confessing our sin and unworthiness. Only then can we consecrate ourselves to the Lord and lay our lives on the altar as those who have let go and are completely surrendered to God. Truly consecrated believers must consider themselves as the absolute property of God, bought and paid for by the precious blood of Jesus according to the will of God.

In conclusion, it is important to remember that the transforming work of the Holy Spirit is continual and should never cease this side of heaven. The goal, as reflected upon earlier in 2 Corinthians 3:18, is to bring about our increasing likeness to the Lord Jesus. That this is possible can never be due to our own ability, or attainments or any form of gifting; it is entirely the work of the Holy Spirit. It is his divine work! With this in mind, it is the believer's responsibility to submit to him in all things and to be sensitive, pliable and self-giving.

In 1 Samuel 10:6 we have a glorious one-phrase description of the transforming work of the Holy Spirit. Although the work of the Holy Spirit in the Old Testament is often on a different basis, we have here a principle that covers both Testaments. Samuel has just anointed Saul as the first king of Israel when he says to him: *The Spirit of the Lord will come upon you in power ... and you will be changed into a different person.* Surely this embodies the wonderful purpose of the gospel, to transform believers into different people, those who are growing increasingly like our blessed Lord Jesus.

May it be our earnest desire to be filled with the Spirit, walk in the Spirit, empowered by the Spirit, and enjoy the God-glorifying experience of being transformed by the Spirit. Herein lies the secret of living 'a normal Christian life'.

In full and glad surrender, I give myself to Thee,
Thine utterly and only and evermore to be.
O Son of God, who lov'st me, I will be Thine alone;
And all I have and am, Lord, shall henceforth be Thine own.
Reign over me, Lord Jesus, O make my heart Thy throne;
It shall be Thine, dear Saviour, it shall be Thine alone.
O come and reign, Lord Jesus, rule over everything!
And keep me always loyal and true to Thee, my King.

Frances Ridley Havergal (1836-79)

11
Worship

The word 'worship' is used in many different ways within the context of church life, sometimes correctly but often incorrectly. Worship is generally associated with music, singing, praise, thanksgiving, praying or communion. Although true worship may be associated with these and other elements, and be part of them, worship is much wider and deeper.

In essence, it is something quite profound. In order to understand what 'normal Christian living' is, it is essential that we grasp the importance and relevance of true worship because worship is not part of the Christian life, it is the Christian life! It is the highest function of the human soul.

What or who is the object of worship? By simple definition, our present-day English word 'worship' comes from the Anglo-Saxon 'weorthscipe' which means 'to attribute worth to something'. Worship means 'worth-ship' i.e. to give someone the honour or worth that is due to their name. Of the many attempts to define worship with some measure of brevity, the following are certainly helpful:

Professor John Murray (1898-1975): 'Worship is the devotion we owe to God in the whole of our lives; there is no area of life where worship should be absent.'

William Temple (1881-1944): 'Worship is the submission of all our nature to God – the nourishment of mind with his truth – the opening of the heart to his love – the surrender of will to his purpose – and all this gathered up in adoration.'

It is clear from these definitions that worship is primarily not so much about what we do but the expression of what we are in relation to God. God created us to be worshippers, it is what we were made for!

Worship ought to be our natural response to God, firstly, because of who he is. He alone is God, there is no other. He is the Creator and Sustainer of all that exists. The first commandment tells us: *You shall have no other gods before me* (Exodus 20:3). Why? Because he says: *I am the Lord your God.*

During his time of temptation, Jesus replied to Satan with these words: *Worship the Lord your God and serve him only* (Luke 4:18). God alone must be the object of our worship, our focus must be centred on him. Whenever we come to worship, if our focus is not God-directed, then whatever it is, no matter how grand, eloquent, loud, appealing or pleasing to our senses, it is not worship.

There is always the great danger of worship being dominated by self, almost a kind of emotional fix, when in reality, true worship is selfless, for only God is in view. A true spirit of worship is almost tangible in the words of John the Baptist: *He must become greater; I must become less* (John 3:30). This was worship drenched in humility!

In the experience of the Apostle Paul, Jesus, the Son of God, once the object of his hatred became the object of his worship. Jesus himself said to Paul (Saul at that time): *Why do you persecute me?* (Acts 9:4). Paul's whole life was turned around from the day of his conversion and Jesus Christ became the sole object of worship. He testified: *For to me, to live is Christ and to die is gain* (Philippians 1:21). His whole life was given over to Jesus his Lord as an act of worship.

Whether it was preaching, praying or suffering, it was all an act of worship. It was his fitting response towards the grace of God and the blessings into which he had entered. Surely this is what Paul has in mind in Romans 12:1, when he says: *Therefore, I urge you, brothers, in view of God's mercy, to offer your bodies as living sacrifices, holy and pleasing to God – this is your spiritual act of worship.*

There are two main Hebrew words for worship. The first is 'hishahawah' and, literally, means 'a bowing down, a prostration before God'. In Psalm 95:6, we read: *Come, let us bow down in worship, let us kneel before the Lord our Maker.* The thought behind this is one of leading God's people to an immediate, deep awareness of the holiness of God and the sinfulness of man. This kind of bowing down is a response to what we are by nature (that is, sinful) and the character of God (which is entirely holy, sinless and righteous). This attitude was seen in action when Peter fell down before Jesus in Luke 5:8, saying: *Go away from me, Lord; I am a sinful man.*

The second Hebrew word is 'abodah' and it means 'service'. True worship is much more than just praising with our lips, it calls for serving with our lives. This thought is expressed in Psalm 116:16, where we read: *O Lord, truly I am your servant.* Worship or service is a response from a grateful heart which manifests itself with a spirit of service. What is worship? It is the bringing of our entire being – heart, will, mind and soul – in total submission and subservience to Almighty God.

Worship that costs nothing is worth nothing! Giving God his rightful place in every part of our lives must, inevitably, prove costly. This was so in the life of Abraham. In Genesis 11 we are introduced to Abraham, a rough, simple sheep-master. He never wrote a book or uttered a prophecy, gave any laws or sang a song, yet his name is echoed throughout God's Word as the father of faith and friend of God.

In Genesis 12, God called Abraham to leave his country, family and friends and to go to another land. Without questioning, he obeyed God's call even though he did not know where he was going. The writer to Hebrews informs us that Abraham *obeyed and went, even though he did not know where he was going* (11:8). God promised him that *all peoples of the earth will be blessed through [him]* (Genesis 12:3).

With the passing of time the miracle of a child called Isaac was born to Abraham and Sarai his wife when they were advanced in years (between 90 and 100 years). The promise of God to Abraham of great future blessing would come through Isaac, this special child of promise. As a means of testing Abraham's faith, God called him to do something that would call for worship at the highest level. One day God said to Abraham: *Take your son, your only son Isaac, whom you love, and go to the region of Moriah. Sacrifice him there as a burnt offering* (Genesis 22:2).

He obeyed, and set out with Isaac to do this. It is not possible to imagine what thoughts occupied Abraham's mind, or for that matter, what Isaac was thinking about as they contemplated what was about to take place. In Genesis 22:5, as Abraham set out to sacrifice his son as a burnt offering, he said to his servants: *Stay here with the donkey while I and the boy go over there. We will worship and then we will come back to you.*

The point in the story is this. Abraham was prepared to sacrifice his only son, the son of promise, as an act of worship! *We will worship*, he said. Not until Abraham had the knife raised in his hand to sacrifice Isaac did God stop him. Until that time he did not know that God would spare his son. However, according to Hebrews 11:17-19, Abraham believed that God could raise his son. True worship may involve sacrifice!

How are we to worship God? The prophet Micah asks the question: *With what shall I come before the Lord and bow down before the exalted God?* (6:6). David Watson comments: 'The church is essentially a worshipping community of those who believe in Jesus Christ. They are called together for this purpose, and to neglect this primary task is to dishonour God and maybe to forfeit his grace and power in all the work that is done in his name.'

Too often worship is seen as a performance, focusing on the feel-good factor of those who are supposedly worshipping. Worship is not a performance! It is not a display of talents and gifts that call attention to those participating, nor is it an emotionally whipped-up gathering. Rather, true worship must always be directed towards the living God. The primary aim of worship is to glorify God and to lead those worshipping into a deeper awareness and sense of the presence of God.

Sadly, the expression often heard from some groups engaging in public worship is, 'Wasn't that a great time of worship' which usually means that they had a good time, loved the music and really enjoyed themselves.

The question is, what did God get from it, not what did we get from it? The worship of the Apostle John stands in contrast to this: *When I saw him, I fell at his feet as though dead* (Revelation 1:17). True worship is selfless and God-focused. Dr Sinclair B Ferguson comments: 'Where God is at the centre of things, worship inevitably follows. Where there is no spirit of worship, there God has been dethroned and displaced.'

The diversity of how we physically express our worship has over the years been a source of contention; indeed, it has unfortunately been the cause of divisions. There are two things to bear in mind. Firstly, we are one body of which Christ is the head. Secondly, we are still individuals with varying emotions and needs. Some will raise their hands, clap their hands, even dance. Others like to kneel, perhaps finding quietness and stillness their preferred choice. Is there a right or wrong way?

In Exodus, following a time when Moses and Israel sang a song, we read of Miriam: *Then Miriam the prophetess ... took the tambourine in her hand, and all the women followed her with tambourines and dancing.* This was acceptable and appropriate at that time. In 2 Samuel 6:14, we read of David: *David wearing a linen ephod, danced before the Lord with all his might.* In Psalms 149:3 and 150:4 we have music and dancing. Raising hands can be found in Psalm 63:4, Lamentations 3:14 and 1 Timothy 2:8. Regarding kneeling or bowing down, there are many scriptural references.

And so, we find varying physical expressions in the Bible. However, the all-important question is not so much, how, but how true, sincere and genuine is our worship? There must be unity amidst diversity. Paul writes: *But everything should be done in a fitting and orderly way* (1 Corinthians 14:40).

Worship that is God-directed must be spiritual worship. The director of true worship is the Holy Spirit. We read in John 16:14 that *he will bring glory to me by taking from what is mine and making it known to you.* Again in John 4:24, Jesus said: *God is Spirit, and his worshippers must worship him in Spirit and in truth.* True spiritual worship will never be chaotic or disorderly; it will edify the body of Christ and be God-glorifying, for we read: *So worship God acceptably with reverence and awe* (Hebrews 12:28). Fleshly worship points to self, spiritual worship points to God. The result of Spirit-filled worship is found in Ephesians 5:18-19, where Paul says: *Be filled with the Spirit. Speak to one another with psalms, hymns and spiritual songs. Sing and make music in your heart to the Lord, always giving thanks.*

Worship may be summed up as the devotion we owe to God in the whole of life. God is interested in every area of life and wants to be sovereign in all things. Christ must be Lord! Paul says as much in 1 Corinthians 10:31, where he writes: *So whether you eat, drink or whatever you do, do it all for the glory of God.* The believer's attitude to worship ought to find expression in every aspect of life. The dominant note from our lives must be that of worship and adoration to God and for this to permeate all of life. Indeed, it is safe to say that when true spiritual worship is in place, all else will find its proper place and level. All our ambitions in life must be subservient to the ultimate and supreme ambition of glorifying God.

12
The power of humility

Who wants to be humble? Is there anything attractive or desirable about humility? What value is there in humility? Have you ever heard anyone say: 'I wish I was humble?' Of all the various qualities sought after in life, humility is not high on the list. In fact, it's probably not even on the list. What does humility mean? The basic secular definition is 'unpretentiousness and lowliness'.

This is certainly not the goal of many in our world today where the common ethos is to think highly of oneself, assert yourself and make your mark in life. Self-worth, self-confidence and self-love are not necessarily wrong, they are compatible with Scripture after all. The great danger, however, is that of self-exaltation.

To the self-righteous Pharisees who were not shy on self-promotion and who made sure that everything they did was for others to see (Matthew 23:5-7), Jesus said: *For whoever exalts himself will be humbled, and whoever humbles himself will be exalted* (Matthew 23:12).

The challenge facing those who are devoted to following Christ is that of the likeness of Christ becoming visible in their lives – the Christian's goal. Paul writes: *And we, who with unveiled faces all reflect the Lord's glory, are being transformed into his likeness with ever-increasing glory, which comes from the Lord who is the Spirit* (2 Corinthians 3:18). When John the Baptist said, *He must become greater; I must become less* (John 3:30), he was saying that for Christ to be more visible in his life he had to become less visible. True humility has no self-recognition.

Andrew Murray writes: 'Humility is that grace that when you know you have it, you've lost it.' More can be achieved for the kingdom of God when self is kept out of the way. Too often the work and glory of God suffers because his children seek the prominent place. When this happens the end product is self-righteousness, not the righteous life that glorifies Christ. When self is on the throne, Christ is off the throne!

No example of humility is greater than that of our Lord Jesus himself. The eternal purpose of God called for humility at the deepest and highest levels through the self-giving of Christ, the Son of God. The incarnation and death of Jesus are surely the most profound and supreme expressions of humility in the history of mankind.

Here was a person whose home was in heaven. He was the object of heavenly worship and enjoyed the sweetness and intimacy of untarnished fellowship with his Father, in an environment free from sin, the dwelling place of God. It was from such a majestic and glorious situation that Christ left to be born as a baby in the lowliest of circumstances. Paul writes: *Who, being in very nature God, did not consider equality with God something to be grasped, but made himself nothing, taking the very nature of a servant* (Philippians 2:6-7).

In obedience to the Father's redemptive purpose, Christ was prepared to release his grasp on all that was his by right and enter this world in a physical way. The surroundings of his birth were humble in the extreme, born in a stable area more suited for animals than the Son of God. Although his birth was endorsed by some unusual people, with shepherds, wise men, angels and a heavenly choir, there was no human grandeur or kingly entourage, no fanfares or crowns!

This is a picture of humility. Christ was born in poverty and reared in obscurity. Until he commenced his public ministry at around thirty years of age, other than his visit to Jerusalem when he was twelve, there is no record of his life or activities. Humility was the hallmark of all that Jesus said and did. His humility is expressed in various ways:

Firstly, it was seen in his silence. During his trial before Pilate, when pressed for answers, we read in John 19:9 that *Jesus gave him no answer*. He did not try to justify or exalt himself. Though he was misunderstood he had no desire to sort them out, their time would come! Peter comments: *When they hurled insults at him, he did not retaliate* (1 Peter 2:23). How difficult this must have been! There is a lesson in this for all believers for there are times, even if you are sure you are right, when the wisest thing for the greater glory of God and your testimony is to remain silent.

Secondly, humility was seen in his service. In John 13:1-17 we have the picture of Christ washing the disciple's feet. Here is the King of kings and Lord of lords performing the role of a servant and slave. The overriding lesson in this passage is that Jesus was showing them an example. He was teaching them the value of humility through the spirit of servanthood, saying: *I have set you an example that you should do as I have done for you. Now that you know these things, you will be blessed if you do them.*

Effective service for our Lord may often be hindered or marred because we want our place, perhaps considering some act of Christian service (supposedly) below our station. Jesus said of himself: *For even the Son of Man did not come to be served, but to serve and give his life as a ransom for many* (Mark 10:45). Paul writes: *And whatever you do, whether in word or deed, do it all in the name of the Lord Jesus* (Colossians 3:17).

There are those who wrongly consider humility to be a form of weakness. The following illustration may help us understand that there is strength and an inner power in true humility: A missionary once told the story of two rugged, powerful mountain goats who met in a narrow pathway joining two mountain ridges. On one side was a chasm 1,000 feet deep, on the other was a steep cliff rising straight up. So narrow was the trail that there was no room to turn around and the goats could not back up without falling. What would they do? Finally, instead of fighting for the right to pass, one of the goats knelt down and made himself as flat as possible. The other goat then walked over him, and they both proceeded safely.

True humility succeeds and accomplishes much more than all our gifts and talents. The Scottish pastor, Robert Murray McCheyne, comments: 'God uses our likeness to Jesus far more than all our gifts and talents.' The kingdom of God is about the righteous life of Christ being on display, not our own righteousness which points only to self. The believer's goal is to leave others thinking about Christ, not themselves! It is all about how wonderful and glorious Christ is!

It is quite remarkable that in order for Christ to demonstrate his redemptive love for us, he had to humble himself in a most degrading, humiliating way. The Apostle Paul describes this: ... *being found in appearance as a man, he humbled himself and became obedient to death – even death on a cross* (Philippians 2:8). Children are born into this world in order to live, but Jesus was born into this world in order to die on a cross. His purpose and mission was to offer up his life and to do so through his self-giving on the cross. From a timeless existence in the heavenly realm with no sin or death, he submitted willingly to death on a cross.

There are three aspects to this act of humility. Firstly, his willingness to give himself up to death in being willing to die for others. Secondly, it was death in the most degrading manner in the form of crucifixion (*even death on a cross*). Thirdly, his death was an act of substitution for he not only paid the price for our sin, more than that, he became that sin and took the punishment that was our due. Peter writes: *He himself bore our sins in his body on the tree* (1 Peter 2:24). Paul writes: ... *though he was rich, yet for your sakes he became poor, so that you through his poverty might become rich* (2 Corinthians 8:9). John Stott sums this up wonderfully, when he says: 'Because of our poverty Christ renounced his riches.'

This is a humility that considers others first, as Paul reminds us: *Do nothing out of selfish ambition or vain deceit, but in humility consider others better than yourselves. Each of you should look not only to your own interests, but also the interests of others* (Philippians

2:3). Paul cites Jesus Christ as the supreme example for all who would bear the name Christian.

Humility must surely be the believer's only response when we consider our Lord in his incarnation and sacrificial giving for all who by nature were lost and without hope. For Christ, it was the way of the cross; for us, it must be the example of the cross. It is only through our humility that Christ will in any way be exalted. If we have any measure of pride or self-exaltation then we hinder the transforming work of the Spirit to make us more like Christ.

C H Spurgeon writes: 'You must grow downwards, that you may grow upwards; for the sweet fellowship with heaven is to be had by humble souls, and by them alone. God will deny no blessing to a thoroughly humbled spirit. When a man is sincerely humble, and never ventures to touch so much as a grain of praise, there is scarcely any limit to what God will do for him. Humility makes us ready to be blessed by the God of all grace, and fits us to deal with one another.'

True humility leaves room for God to work; it clears the way for the Spirit to work unhindered. All our energies and actions must bear the stamp and hallmark of God at work. We can be too big for God to use, but never too small! Referring to Dr Martyn Lloyd Jones' thoughts on church life as he saw it, his biographer Iain Murray writes: 'So much of the activity which he saw in the contemporary religious scene had elements which suggested ambition and the love of power. Self-advertisement and lack of humility in the church he regarded as "the greatest tragedy of all".'

This could not be said of the Apostle Paul, for we read: *I served the Lord with great humility and with tears* (Acts 20:19). His service was a heartfelt response to the God who had forgiven him for all his pre-conversion hatred, abuse and violence towards the church of Jesus Christ. Gratitude for the grace of God was enough to drive Paul on in his ministry, with great humility and tears. What was his ambition? To know more fully the one whom he had previously stood against, as reflected in his aspiration: *I want to know Christ* (Philippians 3:10).

God delights in using smallness and brokenness. Almost without exception we find in Scripture men and women who discovered their usefulness to God, not in their own strengths or abilities, but in their weakness, brokenness and smallness. The list is endless, but among those who stand out are men like Moses. In Egypt he lived in a privileged position within the royal household and was a highly educated and confident man. Yet following his impulsive act of murder he had to flee for his life to the desert region of Midian where he worked as a shepherd for forty years.

Following his forty years in Midian we find a different man. Back in Egypt because of his exalted position he could have said, 'I am the man' ... now, as God calls him to go back as his servant, Moses says: *Who am I?* (Exodus 3:11). Whether it is Moses, Gideon, Peter or many others, we discover the power of humility. *God opposes the proud but gives grace to the humble ... Humble yourselves before the Lord, and he will lift you up* (James 4:6, 10).

Although Paul received the grace of God with enormous gratitude, there were occasions when he was tempted to be proud. He shares his thoughts in 2 Corinthians 12:7-12. In this passage he speaks of being given *a thorn in the flesh*. This thorn, as he calls it, was probably a serious eye illness and he tells us that three times he pleaded with the Lord to have it taken away.

In verses 9-10, we have our Lord's response to Paul: *My grace is sufficient for you, for my power is made perfect in your weakness. Therefore I will boast all the more gladly about my weaknesses, so that Christ's power may rest on me. That is why, for Christ's sake, I delight in weaknesses, in insults, in hardships, in persecution, in difficulties. For when I am weak, then I am strong.* Paul surrendered his circumstances to the Lord and, in so doing, he experienced God's power through his humility.

So then, there is great power in humility for it is a godly disposition that makes us available and useable for the kingdom of God. We become channels or instruments fit for the purpose of God and wanting nothing but the glory of God.

13
Continuing steadfastly

The Apostle Paul writes: *So then, just as you received Christ Jesus as Lord, continue to live in him, rooted and built up in him, strengthened in the faith as you were taught, and overflowing with thankfulness* (Colossians 2:6-7). It is God's purpose for all believers to go on from their spiritual birth continuing in the faith, growing up into spiritual maturity.

Following the birth of a baby it is the normal expectation for it to grow up and develop physically, emotionally and intellectually. Throughout the journey of life there are many demanding and difficult times, hurdles to overcome and challenges to face, such is the case for all people. These are part of normal everyday life.

Likewise, the normal Christian life is full of situations and circumstances that call for perseverance and endurance. The pathway to maturity, our growing up in Christ, is unlikely to be one of ease and free from trial or trouble. Jesus himself said: *In this world you will have trouble. But take heart! I have overcome the world* (John 16:33). As previously discussed in chapter one, Jesus also warned those who desired to follow him that the way ahead would not be easy, and that careful thought should be given by all would-be followers (cf. Luke 14:25-33; Mark 8:34-38).

There are many things in life which are easy to start but difficult to finish. For example, almost anyone could sign up and line up to start a marathon race of more than twenty-six miles, but not all will finish. There may be many reasons why those who started would be unable to finish. It could be fatigue, lack of training, poor tactics or a lack of will-power. Yet even for those who have trained hard, planned their running schedules, worked out their times and pace and looked after their diet, there are still difficult obstacles ahead that will stretch many of them to the limit. Those who run marathons often refer to hitting the wall after having run a good number of miles. At such a time many come to a complete halt, others, however, manage to muster up all their mental and physical energy and press on to finish the race.

The Apostle Paul's second letter to Timothy was probably the last letter he would write before his death. As he does so he recalls the reality of living for Christ. He wrote to Timothy, a young pastor, who needed much encouragement and instruction. Throughout this letter, exhortation after exhortation comes fast and furious to encourage Timothy to continue in the faith and in the ministry. He uses language such as: 'Be strong, endure hardship, remember Jesus, be a workman, do your best, preach the Word and stand your ground.'

In chapter 2, Paul contrasts three different types of people to demonstrate how demanding it can be to continue in the faith. In verses 3-4, he writes: *Endure hardship with us like a good soldier of Christ*

Jesus. No one serving as a soldier gets involved in civilian affairs. Paul suggests that the Christian has to live like a soldier. The soldier lives a life of obedience, he obeys his commanding officer, he endures hardship and does not get caught up in other lesser issues that would distract him from his first responsibility. Just as the soldier wants to please his commanding officer, so likewise, our goal is to please Jesus Christ. We read in Hebrews 12:2, *Let us fix our eyes on Jesus, the author and perfecter of our faith.*

To further emphasise his point, Paul also refers to an athlete and a farmer who bear the hallmarks of endurance (2 Timothy 2:5-6). Both of these would know the discipline and rigour of hard work and training. Dark early mornings, long tedious hours, physical exhaustion or fatigue is common to them. Should they only train or work when they felt like it, then little or nothing would be accomplished. They would not fulfil their intended goal or daily workload.

Looking back over his Christian life, Paul makes three telling statements in 2 Timothy 4:7 which are a wonderful summary of his commitment to the Christian life. He writes: *I have fought the good fight, I have finished the race, I have kept the faith.* A fighter, an athlete and a defender of the faith he certainly was. With every ounce of spiritual and physical energy he served the Lord Jesus Christ. He knew what it was to suffer for the sake of the gospel, even being left for dead on one occasion. Obstacle after obstacle confronted Paul in his endeavours for Christ, sometimes pressures from within the church and also difficulties from without. Throughout times of persecution, ridicule and mistrust Paul continued to live for Christ and preach his name. For a summary of Pauls sufferings see 2 Corinthians 11:23-33.

When we are confronted with difficult times or pressures that make it hard to continue living for Christ, and even when we are tempted to give up, then it's worth remembering that we can turn these to our advantage. Warren W Wiersbe wrote a book called *The bumps are what you climb on*. He demonstrates in this book how we can either allow adverse situations to pull us down or use them as stepping stones to help us move up and on. In the opening chapter, he writes: 'A little boy was leading his sister up a mountain path and the way was not too easy. "Why, this isn't a path at all," the little girl complained. "It's all rocky and bumpy." And her brother replied, "Sure, the bumps are what you climb on." That's a remarkable philosophy. What do you do with the bumps on the path of life? When we bring our bumps before the Lord, he will help us deal with them in such a way that builds us up in the faith.'

No matter how well we understand the nature of Christian living there is the temptation to think that when we are praying, reading, trusting and serving God, that life ought to be good for us. Whilst life is wonderfully joyous at times and we experience the presence and power of Christ, the reality is we live in a world that is set against God and all those who follow him. This is a spiritually dark world and we can expect no favours.

This world witnessed the beauty and glory of God in the person of Jesus; they heard his tender words and saw the miraculous take place before their very eyes, but all they could say was, 'Crucify him, crucify him.' Jesus said: *This is the verdict: Light has come into the world, but men loved darkness instead of light because their deeds were evil. If this world hates you, keep in mind that it hated me first. If you belonged to the world, it would love you as its own. As it is, you do not belong to the world, but I have chosen you out of the world* (John 3:19; 15:18-19).

Essentially, we are called to live a life of faith, as Paul reminds us: *We live by faith, not by sight* (2 Corinthians 5:7). In our journey of faith there will be many testing circumstances. We will come up against situations that are hard to understand and may even cause us to question God. The truth is that adversity and different kinds of troubles are often used by God to sanctify us, shaping and pruning us on the pathway to maturity. Sometimes, it may even be illness. We may plead with God to heal us because we believe God is a God who heals, and he does, but it is not always God's will to heal his children. Christians may feel discouraged and let down at times when God doesn't heal in the way asked for. But God knows what is best! He has the prerogative to act as he chooses. His way is perfect.

In the history of the church and, indeed, throughout Scripture, we find many examples of men and women whom God could have healed immediately and directly, but he chose not to. This is evident in Paul's life as we know from 2 Corinthians 12:1-10 where Paul pleads with the Lord to heal him of some form of illness. The apostle wanted rid of it for life would be easier without it and he could get on with his ministry; but, rather than remove his illness, the Lord said to Paul: *My grace is sufficient for you, for my power is made perfect in weakness* (verse 9).

Paul believed that God allowed this illness to keep him from becoming proud, for he writes: *To keep me from becoming conceited because of these surpassing great revelations, there was given to me a thorn in my flesh* (verse 7). In 2 Corinthians 1:8-9, we have a further example of how when Paul was in a desperate situation, hanging on by his fingertips, that he realised this was to teach him not to rely on his own strength, but on God.

Countless servants of God could testify to God's grace in similar circumstances. I think of Alexander Cruden (1699-1770), well known because of the concordance he compiled based on the King James Version of the Bible, has been described as one who suffered from manic depression. On one occasion C H Spurgeon referred to this man, rather gratuitously, in this way: 'Every day that I live I thank God for half-mad Alexander Cruden.' Throughout his wonderfully gifted ministry God did not remove his illness, but gave him grace to endure it, and that for the glory of God.

God may have many lessons to teach us that call for stickability and perseverance. These lessons are rarely learned when riding on the crest of a wave. No matter how far we have travelled on our spiritual journey, there will always be further to go. It is working through the difficult times relying on God's strength that brings us on to a new level of maturity. This will invariably mean that we have to trust in God, even when we have no idea what's going on. By doing so we are submitting to God's sovereign purpose for our lives.

The normal Christian life is one of discovery, increasingly devoting our lives to Christ and his purpose with a spirit of endurance that is both life changing and God-glorifying. The experience of God's servant Job provides us with a telling and challenging example of his discovery of himself and God. During his period of trial and adversity his faith is tested to the limit. Let's look at this man!

In the book of Job, we see the death of the self-life through the fires of affliction and a new vision of God appearing in Job's life. The self-life with its self-goodness, reason and religion is laid bare for all to see. In Job 1:1, we read: *This man was blameless and upright; he feared God and shunned evil.* Yet in Job 42:6 this same man is found on his face, saying: *Therefore I despise myself and repent in dust and ashes.*

Few men had ever been paid such a compliment by God. In his attitude, he was *blameless and upright.* This does not mean that he was perfect or sinless, but that there were no obvious or glaring sins or blemishes. We are told that he *feared God and shunned evil.* This tells us of his attitude towards sin and wrongdoing for he did not allow sin to creep into his life or temptation to overcome him.

In the opening verses of chapter 1 we are told about Job's wealth, his family, his possessions and his position in society, where we read: *He was the greatest man among all the people of the east* (verse 3). Here we have a picture of a satisfied man. Health, wealth, family, success and religion, what more could he ask for? But it was all about to change! Job became a target for Satan who was allowed by God to bring real tragedy upon him. In one foul swoop Job lost all his wealth and possessions, that was bad; even worse, all of his family were killed, seven sons and three daughters. How did Job respond to such devastation? In a state of deep grief, we read his words: *At this Job got up and tore his robes and shaved his head. Then he fell to the ground in worship and said, 'Naked I came from my mother's womb, and naked I shall depart. The Lord gave and the Lord has taken away, may the name of the Lord be praised'* (verses 20-21).

Job also faced a second test when Satan came before the Lord and suggested that he be further tested. His reasoning was that although Job maintained his spirituality and integrity, it was only because his own flesh had not been touched. Earlier in 1:9, Satan had suggested that Job feared God only because everything in life was good, profitable and pleasant. *Does Job fear God for nothing, he said?* suggesting he feared God only because of what was in it for him. Satan is now given permission by God to further strike Job's own flesh, but with one condition, he must spare his life! So Job was given a terrible skin affliction that drove him almost demented. He had painful sores from the soles of his feet to the top of his head. He used broken pottery to scrape himself in an attempt at finding relief from this relentless irritation.

Most of the book of Job is an almost endless cycle where his closest friends, one after another, suggest that he must have sinned for this calamity to come upon him. They charge him to repent of his sin and get right with the Almighty. No man could go any lower than Job. He was totally isolated and without support. Even his wife said: *Are you still holding on to your integrity? Curse God and die. In all this, Job did not sin in what he said* (Job 2:9-10). Children also mocked him. Forty chapters of statements and counter-statements take place with the Lord himself engaging in the latter stages. During this time Job has some wonderful things to say, such as: *But he knows the way that I take; when he has tested me I shall come forth as gold ... I know that my Redeemer lives* (Job 23:10; 19:25).

Throughout this horrendous affliction, Job knew nothing of Satan's dialogue with God or why all this had befallen him. Yet he surrendered his circumstances to God. He could not understand them or see a way around them, but he kept two eyes on the God of all circumstances, submitting to his sovereign purpose. It is surely beyond us to understand how Job maintained such trust in God. We have, however, a great example and lesson as we seek to continue in the way of faith and trust.

This story would be incomplete without turning to the final chapter. At the outset of Job's story we saw a man who seemed to be in a good place with God, all departments of his life were in order, in particular, his spirituality and worship of God. Yet like Job, most of us have still further to travel in our journey of faith. In Job 42:5, I believe we have one of the most meaningful verses in the whole book, when he says: *My ears had heard of you but now my eyes have seen you.*

As Job reflects on his past he realises that his walk with God at that time was perhaps more shallow and superficial than he understood. It is as though he is now saying, 'Once you were a theory but now you are reality.' What a difference there is between hearing something described and seeing it for ourselves! We may hear the precise detail of some wonderful painting over the phone or read about it in a book, but nothing can be compared to seeing it firsthand. Eugene H Peterson paraphrases Job 42:5-6 in this way: *I admit I once lived by rumours of you; now I have it all firsthand – from my own eyes and ears! I'm sorry – forgive me. I'll never do that again, I promise! I'll never again live on crusts of hearsay, crumbs of rumour.*

Job had one final bump to climb on. After the way his friends had wrongly misunderstood and treated him, God now asks Job to pray for them. Their forgiveness depended on Job's willingness to pray for them, which, remarkably he did. This was the mark of a man who had a new vision of God and who continued and trusted even in the darkest times. After Job had prayed for his friends we are informed that God made him prosperous again, giving him twice as much as he had before. He also had more children and grandchildren. *The Lord blessed the latter part of Job's life more than the first* (Job 42:12).

Job's hardest times proved to be instruments of holiness for they were catalysts to his growth. His suffering smoothed off the rough edges and scraped away the dross. They tested the genuineness of his faith and took him deeper in his relationship with God. Job would not have chosen the way he had travelled but he submitted to it, thereby glorifying God and enriching his own life. Warren W Wiersbe comments: 'Calvary is God's great proof that suffering in the will of God always leads to glory.'

It is unlikely that we should find joy during trials and difficulties, yet in James 1:2-4 we find the reason: *Consider it pure joy, my brothers, whenever you face trials of many kinds, because you know that the testing of your faith develops perseverance. Perseverance must finish its work so that you may be mature and complete, not lacking anything.*

14
Discovering God's will

One of the greatest privileges we have as children of God is that God has a purpose for our lives. He is intimately interested in every part of our being and wants to direct our every step. We are reminded of this in Psalm 139:1-3, where we read: *O Lord, you have searched me and know me. You know when I sit and when I rise, you perceive my thoughts from afar. You discern my going out and my lying down; you are familiar with all my ways.* In this age when men and women, even in their teens, struggle for self-identity and purpose in life, it is quite incredible to think that God has a plan for those who belong to him. How do we know this? Listen to the Word of God:

- *Who have been called according to his purpose* (Romans 8:28)
- *Many are the plans in a man's heart, but it is the Lord's purpose that prevails* (Proverbs 19:21)
- *For I know the plans I have for you* (Jeremiah 29:11)
- *In him we were chosen and predestined according to the plan of him who works out everything* (Ephesians 1:1)

Do we want God's will? Without doubt, God has a plan for our lives, but the question is do we want it? You may think, 'What a strange thing to suggest!' Although we may know in our hearts that God has a purpose for us, it is possible to resist and fight against it. The influence of the old nature often pulls us and we can be tempted to want to do our own thing. Though it may be a struggle at times, doing the will of the Father is evidence that we have entered the kingdom of God and that we are his children, for we read: *Not everyone who says to me, 'Lord, Lord, will enter the kingdom of heaven, but only he who does the will of my Father'* (Matthew 7:21).

On numerous occasions Jesus himself declared that he came to do the will of his Father (John 6:38; Matthew 26:39, 42). In the model prayer taught by our Lord we are instructed to offer our prayers on the basis of the Father's will, *your will be done* (Matthew 6:10). King David, a man after God's own heart, in spite of his failures and struggles, could say: *I desire to do your will, O my God* (Psalm 40:8). Three things for us to consider:

Firstly, discovering God's will calls for our absolute trust. It is so easy to rely on our own sense of direction, wisdom and judgment. The truth is, sometimes we only consult God when our way doesn't seem to be working out. It's not surprising that we read: *Trust in the Lord with all your heart and lean not on your own understanding; in all your ways acknowledge him, and he will make your paths straight* (Proverbs 3:5-6). We are invited to trust him in all our ways, to leave it all to God, no meddling! Dr Sinclair B Ferguson comments: 'The will of God means death to our will, and resurrection only when we have died to all our plans.' Whether it is in difficult and trying circumstances or in the heights of joy, the best place to be is the place where God wants us to be, for in such a place we shall know *the peace of God which transcends all understanding* (Philippians 4:7). God looks for unconditional trust.

Secondly, discovering God's will calls for our desire for God's glory. We must want God to be glorified in all our thoughts, words and deeds. As God's children we are the peak of his creation and it is our responsibility to bring glory to his name. The first question in the Shorter Catechism reminds us of this: 'What is the chief end of man? To glorify God and to enjoy him forever.' Fulfilling God's plan for our lives not only brings glory to his name, it also brings a sense of joy and purpose.

Our goal in life is to complete the work God has given us to do. In Jesus' high priestly prayer to his Father, he said: *I have brought you glory on earth by completing the work you gave me to do* (John 17:4). Is this not a challenge to all who claim to be followers of Christ? Are we set on discovering his will and committed to its completion, thereby bringing glory to his name? On a day yet to come when we stand before our Lord, will we be able to say, 'I have brought you glory by completing the work you gave me to do?'

Thirdly, discovering God's will calls for the crucified life. The Apostle Paul writes: *For to me, to live is Christ and to die is gain* (Philippians 1:21). Here we find Paul in a state of absolute single-mindedness. He wants nothing of his old sinful life to be in evidence, he considers it dead and out of sight (cf. Romans 6:11). And so he says: *I have been crucified with Christ and I no longer live, but Christ lives in me* (Galatians 2:20). Like Paul, we must desire God's will more than anything else, making it our greatest joy to live for his glory, thereby exalting his Son and our Saviour.

Paul's life was so intertwined with Christ's for all that mattered to him was to please him at any cost. Death to the old life must take place in order that God's purpose is not hindered. He writes: *... so that in everything he might have the supremacy* (Colossians 1:18). He never lost sight of the one who loved him and gave himself for him. Elisabeth Elliot writes: 'Acceptance of the will of God means relinquishment of our own. If our hands are full of our own plans, there isn't room to receive his.'

Though there is no better place to be than at the centre of God's will, this does not necessarily ensure an easy path in life; there may be many turns and twists that test and try our faith, ways that at times we do not understand, but his way is best, it is perfect! Paul S Rees writes: 'To understand the will of God is my problem; to undertake the will of God is my privilege; to undercut the will of God is my peril.'

How does God reveal his will to us? God is not restricted in the ways and means through which he communicates his will to us. We read in Hebrews 1:1 that *in the past God spoke to our forefathers through the prophets at many times and in various ways.* Communication between God and his children ought to be a normal ongoing experience. When we pray we speak to God and he hears us, but how does he speak to us? Of the many ways he may choose to reveal his will, the following three are but a sample:

Firstly, God speaks through his Word. When we read, meditate and study his Word, God speaks to us as he brings thoughts to our minds in ways that we recognise as his voice. Of course, we must also be careful that we don't force our will into our mind, convincing ourselves that it is God's voice. That's why we must make sure that we do really want God's will. Only then will we be receptive to hear his voice. In Psalm 119:105, we read: *Your word is a lamp to my feet and a light to my path.* Here we have a twofold application. Firstly, when his Word is a lamp to our feet, it means that through reading his Word he helps us see where we are, to understand our present situation. Secondly, his Word is a light to our path bringing us direction regarding our future for it helps us discern the way ahead.

In Hebrews 4:12 we have a comprehensive description of how the Word operates: *For the word of God is living and active. Sharper than any two edged sword, it penetrates even to dividing soul and spirit, joints and marrow; it judges thoughts and attitudes of the heart.* The Bible is not a lifeless combination of words merely supplying knowledge and information; it is alive and living, breathing out the very purpose of God. *All Scripture is God-breathed and is useful for teaching, rebuking, correcting and training in righteousness* (2 Timothy 3:16). God is able to speak into our innermost being through his Word. He has given his children the ability to understand his voice. When Samuel was just a boy and God was calling to him, he responded by saying: *Speak, for your servant is listening* (1 Samuel 3:10).

Secondly, God speaks through his Spirit. When Jesus was preparing his disciples for the time when he would not physically be with them, he told them about the coming of the Holy Spirit and what his role would be. *But when he, the Spirit of truth comes, he will guide you into all truth. He will speak only what he hears, and will tell you what is yet to come. He will bring glory to me by taking from what is mine and making it known to you* (John 16:13-14).

The Spirit would teach them, he would help them understand the will of God. Paul, in Ephesians 5:15-18, was exhorting the believers to be careful as to how they should live, stressing the need not to be foolish but understand what the Lord's will was. With this in mind, he writes: ... *be filled with the Spirit.* The Holy Spirit would lead and guide them (see chapter eight).

Thirdly, God speaks through circumstances. Very often God speaks to us through events and circumstances outwith our control. It may be a letter, a phone call, a sermon, a book, an adverse situation or something else, perhaps through the wisdom of a friend. God can and does use many different ways and means to speak to us. Normal Christian living calls for a close and sensitive relationship with the Lord, so that in any given situation we are open to hear his voice and discern his will.

What is the reality of God's will? We read in Romans 12:2 (J B Philips translation): *That you may prove in practice that the plan of God for you is good, meets all his demands and moves towards the goal of maturity.* Although at times we may struggle with its acceptance, God's will is and always will be good for us. We may question it, not fully understand it, even resist it, but God knows what he is doing. It is not only good for us, but when we give ourselves wholly to it and want nothing else, it is a means of taking us on to maturity.

We are also reminded from Romans 8:28 that *in all things God works for the good of those who love him.* God is able to use any and every situation for his glory and purpose. Only when we truly love God are we able to submit to *all things,* believing the words of Job: *I know that you can do all things; no plan of yours can be thwarted* (42:2).

Ultimately, there is no better way for the believer than the way chosen for him by God. It is better to be in a battleground than a playground and be at the centre of God's purpose. A life of ease may seem a comfortable place to be at times, but that's not necessarily where we will discover God's purpose.

From Judges 6-7 we learn about Israel's struggle during a period of disobedience when they had strayed from the purpose of God. But God had not stopped loving them or deleted them from his purpose, and so one day while Gideon was threshing out wheat in a winepress for fear of the Midianites, God spoke to him. The angel of the Lord said to him: *The Lord is with you, mighty warrior* (6:12). Gideon's response is perhaps typical: *If the Lord is with us, why has all this happened to us? Where are all his wonders that our fathers told us about?* (6:13). At that time Israel were insensitive to the purpose of God, they had tried to do things their own way, which only ended up in failure and defeat.

The time was now right for God to raise up Israel, and in so doing he called on Gideon to lead his people. The Lord referred to Gideon as a *mighty warrior,* which he was not at that point in time, but that is what he would later become. The narrative tells the story of how God prepared Gideon to place fresh trust in him, eventually leading his people to victory. It was God's purpose that his people would be victorious, yet Gideon made excuse after excuse, suggesting to God that he was not the right man.

In 6:15, he says: *How can I save Israel? My clan is the weakest in Manasseh and I am the least in my family.* But the Lord said to Gideon: *I will be with you* (6:16). Gideon would eventually lead Israel to a glorious victory, but not by their own strength, only God's! He would experience the purpose of God, but only following his commitment of faith. When God's children are in the right place, his presence will always be with them.

Gideon and Israel had to learn that God's way called for complete trust and obedience. The story began with Gideon questioning the purpose of God. He was saying to God: 'If you really are God and have a purpose for us, why are all these bad things happening to us?' The truth was they had wandered from the purpose of God through disobedience and lack of trust. Israel had tried to go it alone as they had done on numerous occasions, without success. The reality of God's purpose for them meant that they must renew their trust, no matter the circumstances.

It is often easy to see the hand of God in retrospect. This is certainly true as we glance at the life of Joseph. His story begins in Genesis 37 when he is just 17 years old. The story is well known. Joseph with his dreams and spoiled childhood, his multicoloured coat and the favourite of his father, all became the source of contention and hatred of his brothers.

From this time until Joseph was the governor of all Egypt, much had happened. He was thrown into the pit, then pulled out and sold as a slave into the family of Potiphar. In that household he gained promotion and conducted himself well until he is framed by Potiphar's wife for rape. He is thrown into prison. Once again, he did well and gained promotion, being put in charge of other prisoners. The pit, Potiphar's house and the prison cover a period of thirteen years. During that time, what must Joseph have been thinking about? Perhaps, 'Where is my God? Why has he allowed all these things to happen?'

Several times during those years we read that *the Lord was with Joseph*. We could well ask, 'If the Lord had been with him, why did he let these situations take place? Where was justice?' The truth is, although Joseph did not understand what was happening, God was doing something with his life. These were years of preparation for a position and responsibilities that Joseph could never have dreamed of. Not only did he and his family's future depend upon this, but the whole future development of the nation of Israel which was yet to emerge, hinged upon God's plan. Joseph's gifts and God-given abilities were all used for the furtherance of God's purpose, but only when he was ready to use them. It was so important that Joseph remained faithful during those trying, uncertain years.

Eventually, his father and family arrived in Egypt. Joseph sought no revenge against his brothers for the way they treated him many years before, even allowing his father to think that he had been killed, how cruel was that? Joseph forgave them. They had been in Egypt for a number of years when his father died. At that time, his brothers (although Joseph had forgiven them years before) thought that Joseph would now get even with them since his father was out of the way.

It is at this point in the story that we have one of the most touching phrases in all Scripture when Joseph said to his brothers: *Don't be afraid. Am I in the place of God? You intended to harm me, but God intended it for good to accomplish what is now being done* (Genesis 50:19-20). Joseph may have been in prison for many years, but God was at work!

God's will should not be hastened or rushed. If you force the opening of a rose you will crush it, if it unfolds in its own time it will be beautiful and fragrant. God works out his purpose in his way and in his time. The will of God for our lives depends on our continued trust and obedience in any and every situation, whether we understand what is happening or not. Surrendering daily to his will and purpose is not simply our duty, it is our greatest privilege. Discovering the life that God has planned for us depends upon this.

THE WILL OF GOD
Nothing more – Nothing less – Nothing else

15
Pathway to holiness

I f you were asked, 'Are you a holy person?' what would you say? Would you respond with, 'O no, I have a long way to go before I dare consider myself to be a holy person?' Do you think that holiness is something beyond you and that you would only associate holiness with a minority of people, those whom you consider to be very gracious, godly and pious, almost saint-like? Most Christians would never dream of thinking that they are holy people. A W Tozer writes: 'We have learned to live with un-holiness and have come to look upon it as the natural and expected thing.' This is, of course, the crux of the problem.

The truth is that holiness and normal Christian living are inseparable for 'normal Christian living' ought to be 'holy Christian living'. This helps us understand why in my preface I quoted Watchman Nee: 'What is the normal Christian life? It is something very different from the life of the average Christian.' The assumption is that many Christians are living below par. If this is the case, and I suggest it is, it means that a lot of Christians may not be experiencing the quality of life God intended for them:

I have come that they may have life, and have it to the full (John 10:10).

How are we to define holiness? Holiness is a word used to describe the character of God. The prophet Isaiah cries out: *Holy, holy, holy is the Lord Almighty* (6:3). Then in Revelation 15:4, we read: *For you alone are holy.* Scripture affirms clearly that God is holy. The Greek word is 'hagios' and it means 'set apart or devoted to special use'. God is set apart. In Hebrews 7:26, we read that our Lord is *set apart from sinners, exalted above the heavens.* This is why the incarnation of Jesus is an almost unthinkable event. By nature Jesus is set apart, entirely without sin, pure, holy and perfect in every way, yet he took upon himself human flesh and mingled freely with humanity.

Holiness is quite the opposite of every form of sin and evil. The prophet Habakkuk in 1:13, writes: *Your eyes are too pure to look on evil; and cannot tolerate wrong.* This helps us understand why our Lord Jesus cried out on the cross: *My God, my God, why have you forsaken me?* (Mark 15:34). At that time Jesus was the bearer of our sin; he became sin taking the full-blown weight, burden and penalty of our sin upon himself. The Apostle Peter puts it this way in his first epistle: *He himself bore our sins in his own body on the tree* (2:24). As our Lord hung upon the cross, his Father had to turn away his gaze so that he could not look on his own Son. God could not look upon sin. This is why our Lord cried out in such deep anguish and with a sense of utter isolation.

Now then! Although quite beyond our understanding, it is God's purpose that we share in his holiness. This is the miracle of salvation. Listen to what Scripture has to say about this:

- *For he chose us in him before the creation of the world to be holy* (Ephesians 1:14)
- *He ... has saved us and called us to a holy life* (2 Timothy 1:9)
- *I am the Lord who makes you holy* (Exodus 31:9)
- *That we may share in his holiness* (Hebrews 12:10)
- *Be holy because I, the Lord your God, am holy* (Leviticus 19:2)

It is a hard thing to understand that God calls us to be what he is in terms of holiness. Yet this is God's mandate for all his children. This must be the goal and requirement for all who know Christ. It makes no difference whether they are wise or foolish, rich or poor, master or servant, old or young, professors or pastors.

In Hebrews 12:14, we read: *... without holiness no one will see the Lord.* What does this mean? The original readers of this letter understood the preparations necessary for temple worship. They had to be ceremonially clean or holy in order to enter the temple and experience God's presence. Apart from outward washing, their hearts and minds had to be prepared. The same idea is found in Psalm 24:3-4, where we note: *Who may ascend the hill of the Lord? Who may stand in his holy place? He who has clean hands and a pure heart.*

The pathway to holiness calls for a separation from sin. Sin will always block or cloud our vision of God. Too often a sense of God's holy presence is lost in our worship because of the need for inner cleansing. It was to mature Christians that the Apostle John wrote: *If we confess our sins, he is faithful and just and will purify us from all unrighteousness* (1 John 1:9). Confessing our sins is the sure way to come clean before God. God does not call us to separate ourselves from the world for he wants us to be in the world, but to be separate from sin. A prerequisite to holiness is a heart that wants to be separate from sin. Holiness makes us more fit for the presence of God and more useful for God in this sinful world.

Holiness is thoroughly practical. It is not some pie in the sky concept found in total isolation. The truth is that holiness is to be discovered at the coal face of life, separated unto God, yet rubbing shoulders with sinful men and women who are loved by God and need salvation. One of the last things our Lord did before he ascended to heaven was to command his disciples to go into all the world. They were to be salt and light amidst an unholy and dark world; a holy people with the message of a gospel of transformation.

The state of holiness is to be in a place where we want only what God wants, where to please him in all things is what matters most to us in life. It is the surrendered heart and mind to the sovereign purpose of God. Holiness is not to be found in mere knowledge or profession, it is to be discovered and nurtured in the battlefield of life where God's children take their stand for all that is right and righteous. It is not to be had without a fight. That is why, you may recall from chapter 14, that Paul speaks of fighting, running and wrestling. True Christianity is always a fight!

In his wonderful book entitled, *Holiness*, Bishop J C Ryle (1856-1925) wrote the following: 'The true Christian is called to be a soldier, and must behave as such from the day of his conversion to the day of his death. He is not meant to live a life of religious ease, indolence and security. He must never imagine for a moment that he can sleep and doze along the way to heaven, like one travelling in an easy carriage. If he takes his standard of Christianity from the children of this world, he may be content with such notions; but he will find no countenance for them in the Word of God. If the Bible is the rule of his faith and practice, he will find his course laid down very plainly in this matter. He must "fight". The principal fight of the Christian is with the world, the flesh and the devil. These are his never dying foes.'

At the time when the Apostle Peter wrote his letters, the believers were under persecution and the challenge he brought to them was not so much how to survive, but something quite different. He asked an all-important question, relevant for all time and never more so than today: *What kind of people ought you to be? You ought to live holy and godly lives* (2 Peter 3:11). Nothing is more powerful than a holy life! Why? Because it regulates our every thought, word and deed. In every avenue of life, the holy person stands out as one separated unto the Lord. Words can be meaningless, indeed, they can be evidence of our hypocrisy if our lives don't match up to them. What is our response to this question? What kind of people are we? Are we living holy and godly lives?

What we are before God is the all-important thing. We are reminded from Ephesians 1:4 that God called us even before creation that we should be holy. Before we were even born, God determined in his heart that on a future day he would draw us to himself through salvation, and why? To be holy! That's how mega important holiness is!

The pathway to true holiness demands our consecration and resolve to give ourselves wholly to the Lord. This means nothing less than submitting every fibre of our being to God. Men and women may disagree with our message or opinions, they may debate the finer points of theology or stand against us with great atheistic vehemence, but they cannot argue with a changed life.

The one thing Christians must not do is browbeat themselves, perhaps feeling a hopeless sense of inadequacy as though holiness is something unreachable and unattainable. Be sure of this, the pathway to holiness will always be unattainable if we rely on our own resources and strength. When our dependence is upon the Lord and the working of his Spirit and we have settled in our hearts to walk according to his purpose, then and only then can true holiness be the hallmark of our lives. This ought to encourage us!

What is the starting place for the pathway to holiness? We must discover, or rediscover the discipline of personal devotions, where we communicate daily with our Father in prayer, praise and worship, simply enjoying being in his presence. It is significant that during his earthly ministry our Lord often took his disciples with him to a place of prayer. Taking them away from the hustle and bustle of a busy day to a place of quietness and privacy where they could be alone with their heavenly Father. To be in his presence, even in silent submission to his person and purpose and just appreciating being in his company, is the seedbed for holy living. What better company could we possibly have than the Lord's?

The Word of God must also have a genuine priority in our lives. We must feed our hearts and minds from this treasure-trove of inexhaustible manna from heaven. There is no book like it, for it is God's Word from beginning to end. If we are to experience something of the holy life which God has ordained for all true Christians, the Bible must be our constant source of nutrition.

Finally, it is knowing God and growing in the knowledge of God that is the key which will take us beyond the mediocrity that has so characterised the church of our age. The life worth living is only to be discovered when God has his rightful place in our lives. Real joy and soul satisfaction come through a healthy relationship with our Lord. When God is in the right place in our lives, then we are in the right place!

A W Tozer writes: 'To enjoy this growing knowledge of God will require that we go beyond the goals so casually set by modern evangelicals. We must fix our hearts on God and purposefully aim to rise above the dead level and average of current Christianity.'

May God help us all to live the transformed life and be partakers of his holiness. *Be holy because I, the Lord your God, am holy'* (Leviticus 19:2).